KEEP CREATING ANYWAY

By Nina Barr

Hand-Drawn Illustrations By Nina Barr

eBook: 9781807210205
Paperback: 9781807210212
Hardback: 9781807210229

Table of Contents

Start Anywhere

A note from me to you

— about what it means to begin, again and again

Part I:
Becoming of Me

"Every artist was first an amateur." - *Ralph Waldo*

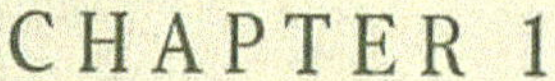

CHAPTER 1

The Girl from Florida

A look at where I was born and raised,
and the sunshine roots that shaped me.

Art came back.
Photography came back.
And I came back — to myself.

~

I was born in Wellington, Florida, at Palms West Hospital – a true Florida girl through and through. Raised out near Indian Mound, I spent my childhood between horse barns, sandbars, and schoolyards.

From an early age, I was the kind of kid who wanted to try everything – I rode horses, played soccer and volleyball, and even went to cheer camp once. But Florida wasn't just about sports and sunshine. It was also about saltwater and stillness – **boating with my family, snorkeling under the surface, finding beauty in the water and sky.**

And then came the brush.

My love for creativity started somewhere quieter. My grandmother, on my mother's side, gave me my very first coloring book and pack of drawing utensils – a brush, a pencil. I don't even remember what she said that day – I just remember never wanting to put them down. Art became my first language, and I never stopped speaking it.

And somewhere in that same season of life, another love quietly rooted itself: horses.

Our first horse was named Duchess – a small, blind miniature pony with a heart of gold. She wasn't fast or flashy, but she was mine. My grandfather, Poppy, brought her home to live on the family ranch, and from the moment I met her, I was hooked. She had a nose for carrots and apples, and I had a knack for brushing her mane and making up imaginary pony rides. I'd spend hours by her side, watching, learning her rhythm. That bond – between girl and pony – planted something permanent in me.

The Driftwood Tradition

Every summer, to celebrate the Fourth of July, we'd pack up and head to Florence, Alabama – the place where my dad grew up. We spent our summers on the water: jet skiing, tubing, fishing, and painting driftwood we'd find in the cove (or "slu," as we called it). Hobby Lobby runs were part of the tradition too – I'd stock up on paints and brushes, ready to turn those lake leftovers into art.

There was so much history in Florence. My dad's childhood home – the house where my grandparents lived their whole lives – became the backdrop of so many memories. That household was full of generations, laughter, and legacy. Even now, I can still picture it. Still feel it.

Florence taught me about freedom, family, and the kind of summer that stains your skin with joy and your heart with gratitude.

Back in Florida, I bounced through three elementary schools in Wellington, one middle school, and eventually made my way west – all the way to the Glades – where I graduated high school in 2011.

The Driftwood Tradition

We spend our summers by the water, engaging in activities like jet skiing, tubing, and fishing. We also njoy painting driftwood we discover in the lake, while sharing laughter and stories on the porch.

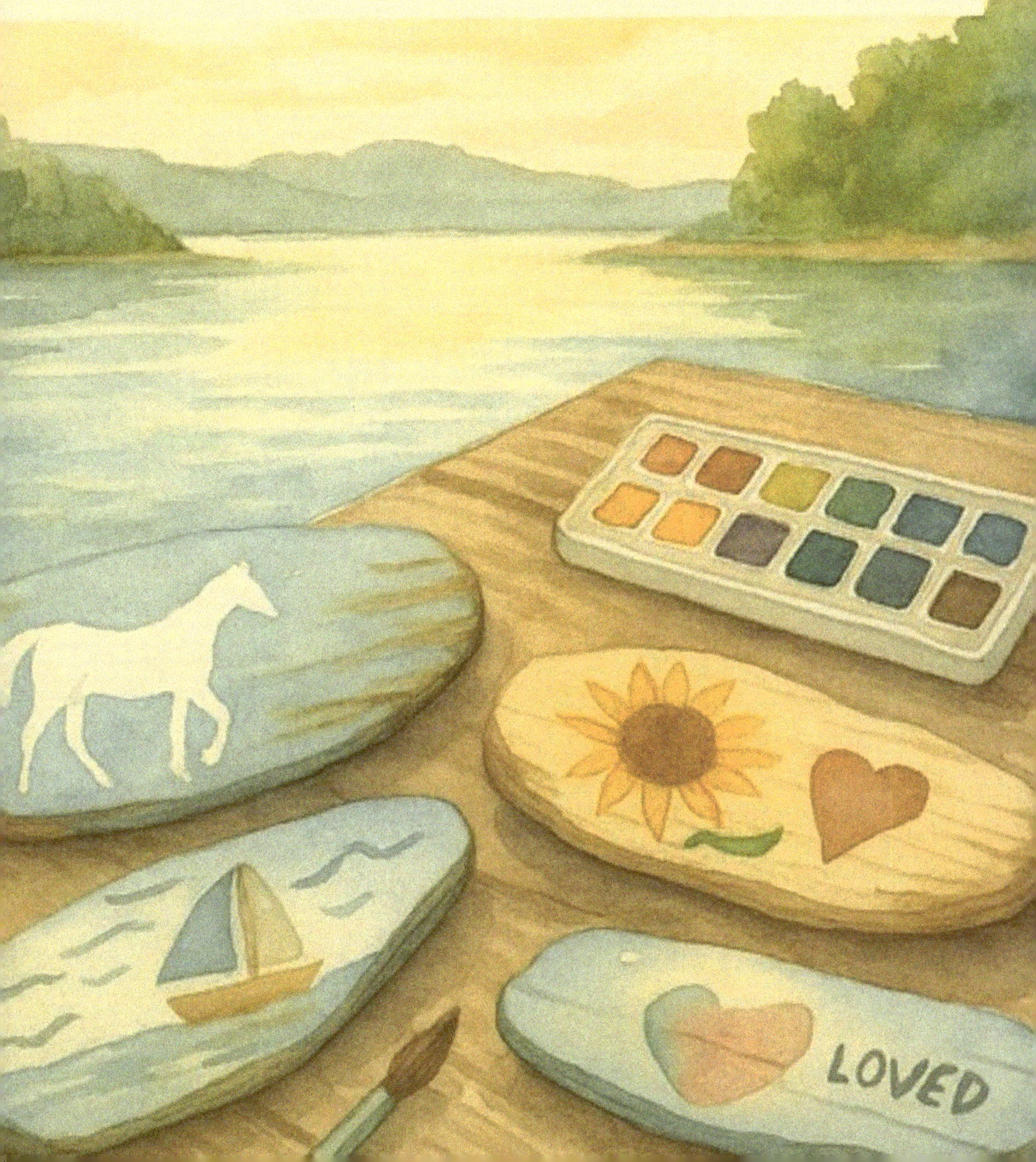

Then I applied to Mississippi State University with one goal in mind: to study art, with a focus on photography. I got in. I left home. I found new people, new places, and a deeper meaning of myself in those years. But plans changed – and so did my major. I graduated with a bachelor's degree in Interdisciplinary Sciences, focusing on kinesiology, psychology, and business.

Funny how life cycles back – because now, my true passion is right where I started: art and photography. I probably should've just stuck with it from the start. But maybe that winding road was necessary.

I thought my creative life would begin there. But life has a different way of painting your timeline.

After college, I returned to Wellington and took a job with Equestrian Sport Productions (ESP), where my love for horses met my love for events and visuals. It felt like a great fit – until COVID hit. Suddenly, the world shut down, and like many others, I was let go when the company downsized.

That's when my dad called and asked if I could help with **Madsen Barr Corporation**, our family's underground construction company. I said yes.

At first, I worked behind the scenes – managing books, payroll, financials, and anything to keep things moving. But slowly, creativity crept back in: I began helping with marketing, brand direction, storytelling, social media, and visuals. Even in a world of pipes and permits, I was still an artist at heart.

Now, I continue to support Madsen Barr as Executive VP – while also building my own dream: **Nina Barr Studio**, where I blend photography, fine art, and brand development. I help tell stories across equestrian, coastal, and lifestyle worlds.

Funny how life works, isn't it? Art always finds a way back.

"If you love something, let it go. If it comes back, it's yours."

Art came back.

Photography came back.

And I came back – to myself.

CHAPTER 2

College, Coffee, and Camera Rolls

My path through school and how I found focus—through trial, error, and a lens.

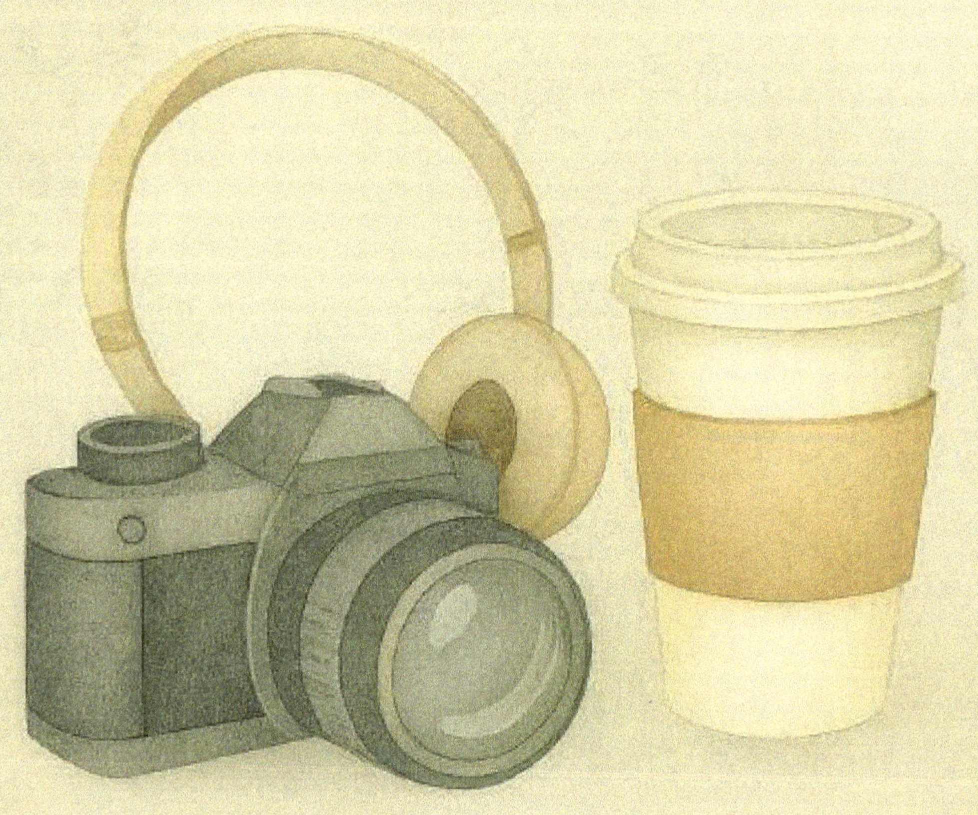

and self-doubt

Didn't Ruin Me

~

I started college the way a lot of people do: undeclared, unsure, and quietly hoping I'd figure it all out before graduation day.

I remember sitting in a crowded lecture hall, surrounded by students who already seemed to have it all together – pre-med majors, future attorneys, finance bros in polos who knew where they were headed. Meanwhile, I was sipping iced coffee, silently wondering if anyone else was just... floating.

My dream growing up was to be a **veterinarian**. I've always loved animals – cows, horses, dogs, all of them. But somehow, between science class and the idea of 8+ years of school, I realized that wasn't my path. I even thought about switching to **vet tech**, but that felt like cheering from the sidelines when I knew I wanted to be on the field creating.

Peanut Gallery Opinions

The peanut gallery (you know the type) was always there, tossing out their unsolicited advice:

"You can't make money with art."

"Photography is just a hobby."

"Pick something safe, something real."

And for a while, I listened. I tried to blend in, pick a major, rush a sorority, and flow with the formula.

College gave me new people, new places, and yes – some unforgettable memories. But it also gave me this ache in my chest. I felt like I was trading in pieces of myself just to check all the boxes.

The Missed Lens

I had a camera. I had sketchbooks. I had this pull toward something more expressive. But I kept it quiet, hidden under coursework and weekend plans.

Looking back now, I wish I'd leaned into photography and art from the start. Not because I'd be further ahead – but because I would've spent more time aligning with who I really am.

But Maybe That Was the Lesson

Maybe I needed to drift a little.

Maybe I had to feel what it was like to be off-track so I could really appreciate finding my way back.

And I did find it again – through practice, persistence, and a whole lot of passion.

Now I know:

This is what I was meant to do.

And no major, no classroom, no comment from the peanut gallery can take that away from me.

So here I am.

A little older, a little wiser, and still chasing the light through the lens.

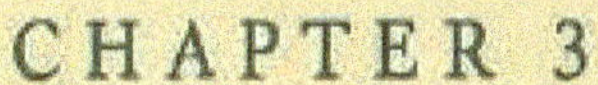

CHAPTER 3

The Art of Slowing Down

Discovering stillness, art, and a deeper way of seeing the world.

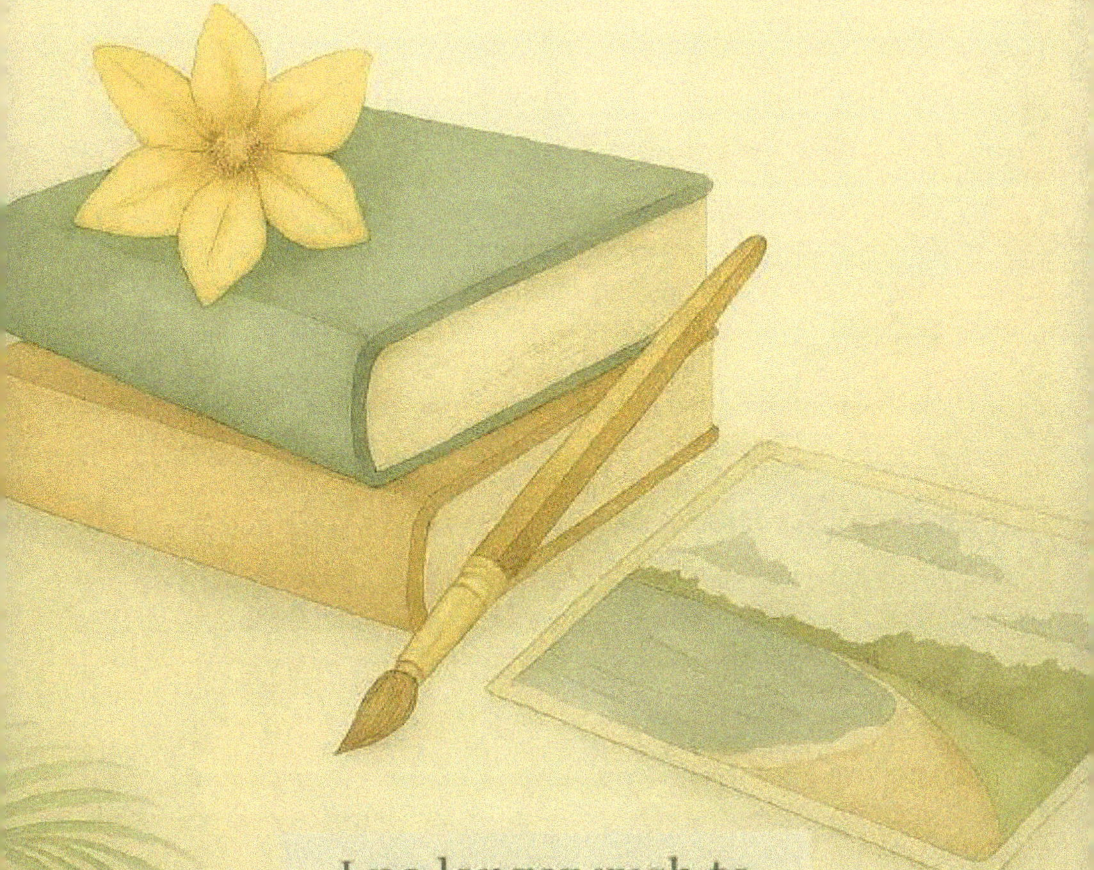

I no longer rush to check off items on my list since that time.

~

The world moves fast – like, really fast.

People scroll instead of pausing. Hustle instead of observing. Rush through tasks, relationships, even sunsets.

But me? I've always seen life a little differently. I see in color.

Bright, Messy, Beautiful Color

When I paint, I use bold colors – layered, loose, unapologetically bright. Some people say my work still needs refining. Maybe it's not gallery-perfect yet. But to me? Each piece is a moment. A pause. And a deep breath turned into something visual.

I paint slowly. Sometimes stroke by stroke. Dot by dot. And that's okay. That's where meaning lives.

Don't Rush the Sunset

The best things in life don't come quickly. A good photograph takes light and timing. A great painting takes layers. Even a sunset needs the patience of a few minutes to shift from gold to pink to violet.

And it's the in-between where the real magic happens.

So I take my time, I snap a photo, then paint it. I don't try to capture it perfectly – I try to feel it.

Mistakes are Human, and That's the Point

I'm not here to preach, but I do believe in grace. We all mess up. We all move too fast sometimes. Say the wrong thing. Choose the wrong color. Miss a detail.

But the beauty is: you get to go back. Fix it. Learn. Try again.

That's what art teaches you. And maybe that's what life and faith are about too – knowing you're human, giving yourself grace, and starting again. Every day is a blank canvas if you let it be.

Slowness Is Power

Taking life slowly doesn't mean being lazy. It means being **present**. It means catching the little things – like the sound of birds in the morning or the way a horse's ear flicks when it listens. It means hearing the music. Savoring your coffee. Doing your job well, not fast.

When you slow down, people notice. They feel your energy. They respect the care you bring to what you do.

And over time, success does this funny thing – it stops running ahead of you and starts walking beside you.

So here's my advice:

Paint slow.

Live slow.

Love slow.

Take it all in, and trust that beauty is waiting for you in every patient breath.

Part II:
Building From Scratch

"The best way to predict the future is to create it." – *Peter Drucker*

CHAPTER 4

YOU'LL NEVER MAKE MONEY DOING THAT

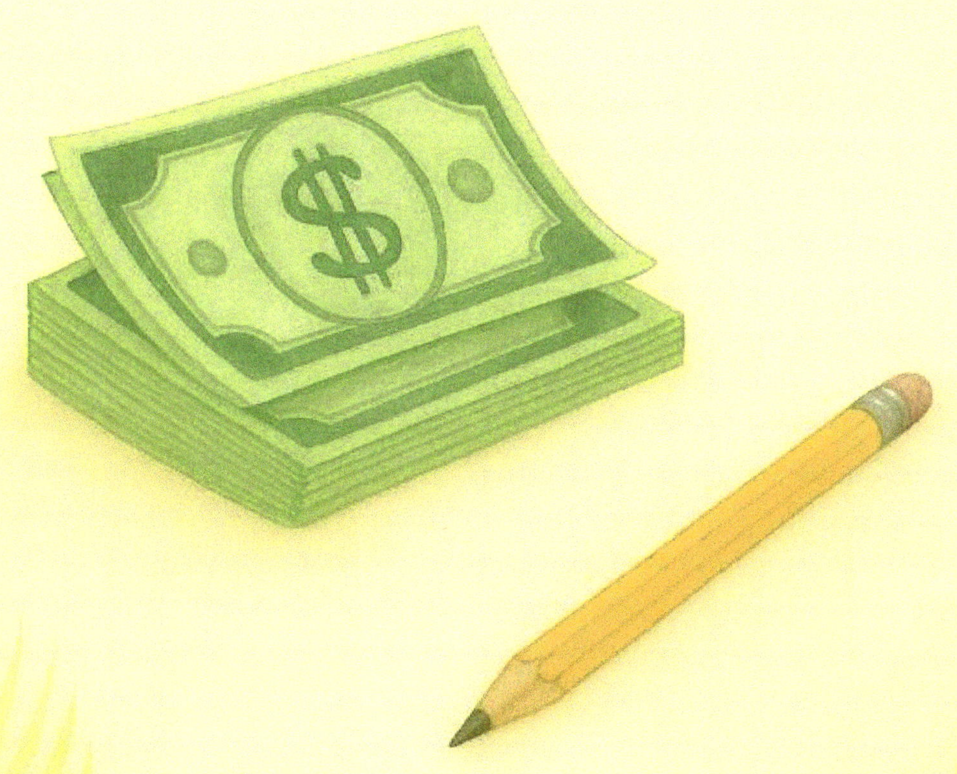

The things they said,
the life I'm building anyway

~

There's always someone ready to tell you that your dream isn't realistic. For me, it usually sounds like:

"You'll never make money doing that."

"Photography is a hobby, not a career."

"Art is cute, but what's your real job?"

They say it with a smirk. Or a laugh. Or worse – fake concern dressed up as advice.

But let me ask this:

Have they ever seen a *National Geographic* cover and not been moved?

Do they know the name Guy Harvey?

Because people like that have made **art** their legacy. Their impact. Their living.

So, why not me?

That's the question that kept nudging me forward. If they could do it, why couldn't I?

I may not have a big gallery show (yet).

I may not shoot for global publications (yet).

I may not be on the *Today Show* as a best-selling author (yet).

But I am showing up. Every single day.

With persistence.

With consistency.

With vision.

And that's more than most people can say.

Not About Trust – About Timing

I used to think I needed others to believe in me to move forward. But I don't.

I need to believe in myself.

The truth will come.

The audience will grow.

The collectors, the buyers – they will show up eventually.

But first? You have to keep going – even when all you hear is your own breath.

Slower Than You Think – But Better That Way

Success doesn't explode overnight. It blooms – like wildflowers in a field you forgot you planted.

Sucess doesn't explode overnight
It blooms – like wildflowers on a
field you forgot you planted

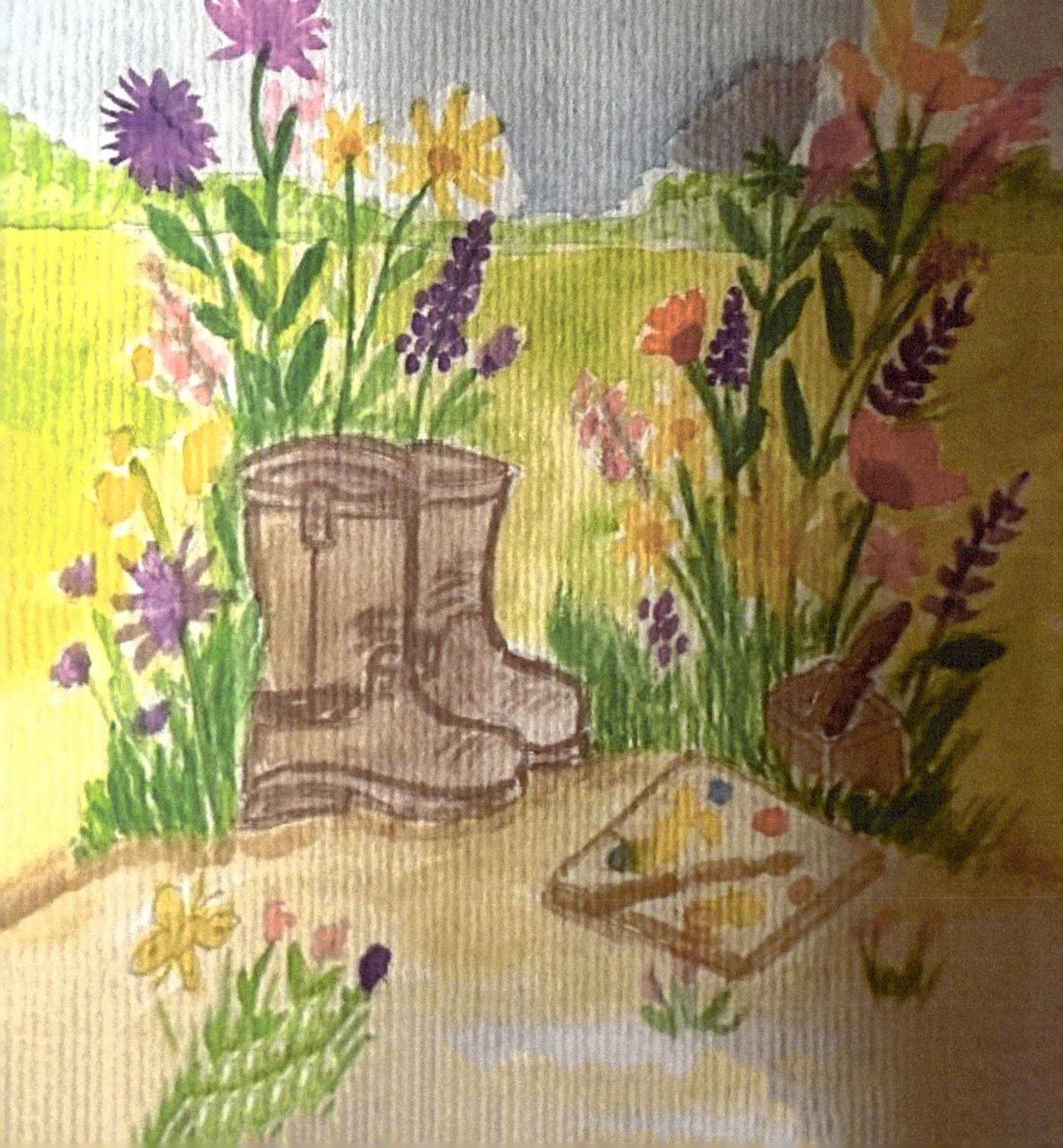

I learned that in Chapter 3. The slower you go, the more clearly you can see. And the more clearly you see, the more powerful your work becomes. So maybe I will be a millionaire tomorrow. But I'll be fulfilled. And with time, that fulfillment turns into real, tangible success.

Because this is my dream. And I'm going to keep showing up—camera in hand, brush in grip, heart wide open. So, to the ones who said I'd never make money doing this?

Just watch.

CHAPTER 5

PRACTICE, PATIENCE, AND PAINTBRUSHES

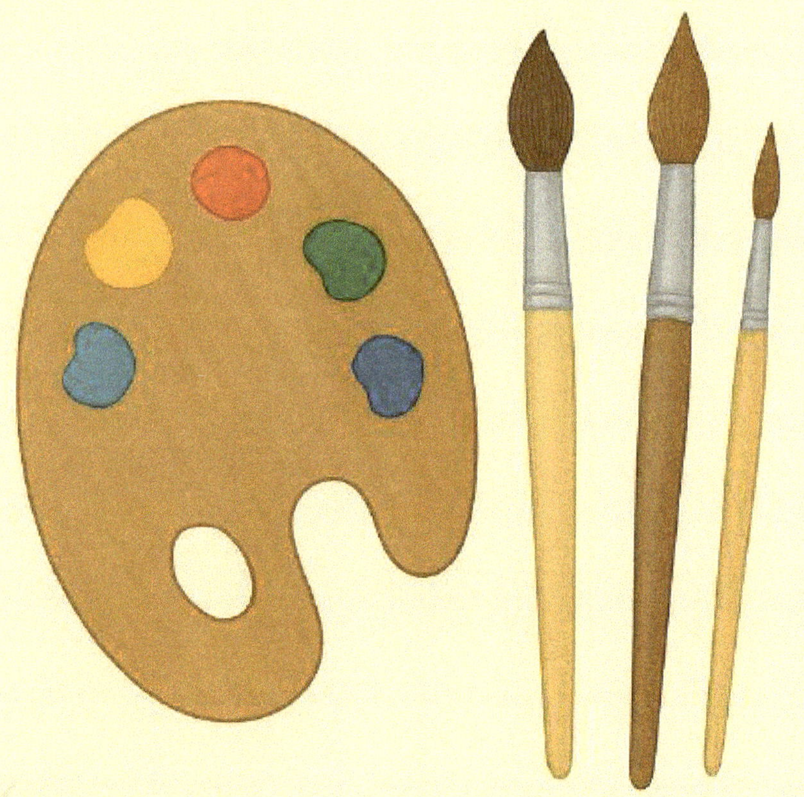

What they don't teach you in business school: why practice is everything

~

If there's one phrase I've come to live by, it's this:

Practice your art. Have patience.

No one teaches you that in school—especially not in business school.

You're taught to chase goals, meet metrics, and grow fast.

But what if real growth looks more like a slow sketch than a perfectly measured spreadsheet?

Start the Day, or Start in the Afternoon

Artists aren't always 5 a.m. hustlers. Sometimes we wake up slowly, drink coffee a little too long, and finally pick up the brush or camera mid-afternoon when the light feels just right.

And that's okay.

There's no perfect schedule for creativity.

The key is to just start—even if you're not ready.

Even if it might not come out exactly how you pictured it.

Make Mistakes. And Then Make Art Out of Them.

You're going to color outside the lines.

The paint might run.

Your photo might be blurry.

But who's to say it isn't still art?

Art is expression. It's emotion in motion.

And sometimes the messiest pieces become the most honest.

That's why I try new things—different brushes, mediums, textures.

Because even if the outcome isn't perfect, the act of creating is where the magic lives.

The Power of Practice

Here's what practice really means:

- Showing up again and again, even when no one's watching.
- Building muscle memory through repetition.
- Growing your own style—not copying someone else's.
- Pushing through the days when inspiration feels completely out of reach.

It's hard.

But it's also how we grow—not just as artists, but as people.

Patience Isn't Passive. It's Power.

Patience is what keeps you grounded when your work isn't moving at the pace you hoped.

It teaches you to:

- Appreciate the process, not just the outcome.
- Let go of perfection.
- Avoid comparing your Chapter 2 to someone else's Chapter 20.
- Find joy in the rhythm of slow creation.

It's why I love psychology, too.

In college, I minored in it—and I loved learning about how the mind works, how people heal, and how patience is the foundation of real understanding.

A psychologist listens, observes, waits.

And so does an artist.

Even Picasso Had Practice Days

Picasso didn't become Picasso overnight.

He practiced. He experimented. He failed.

He tried something bold, and then tried again.

Behind every masterpiece is a stack of work that didn't quite make it.

Creating Is Like Gardening

Think of it like this:

Art is a garden.

You plant the seed. You water. You wait.

Some things bloom right away. Others take time.

But if you keep tending to it—with care, patience, and belief—it will grow.

Final Thought

This chapter isn't about being perfect.

It's about showing up and not giving up.

Because maybe one day, someone will hang your work on their wall.

Maybe it'll end up in a gallery.

Maybe it won't.

But it will still matter—because you made it.

And you made it with patience, purpose, and love.

"Do not go where the path may lead; go instead where there is no path and leave a trail." – Emerson

CHAPTER 6

REDEFINING SUCCESS

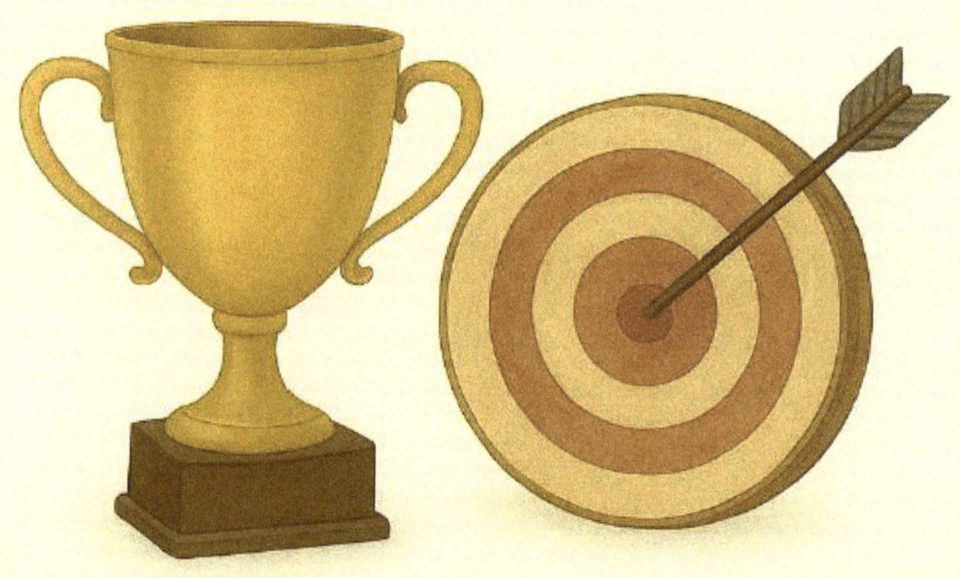

Not fame, not fortune
– but fullfillment

~

Success used to mean a big job title. A certain number in the bank account. Followers. Recognition. Approval.

But if you've made it this far into this book, you already know:

That's not what success looks like for me anymore.

Success is waking up excited to do what you love.

Success is putting in the practice, trusting the process, and seeing progress—even if it's slow.

Success is staying true to your passion, even when others doubt it.

The World Told Me It Wasn't Enough

People have said things like:

"You'll never make money doing that."

"Art is just a side thing."

"Photography isn't a career."

But let me ask you this:

Is something only valuable if it makes millions?

Is it only successful if it goes viral?

No.

Real success is internal first. It's quiet before it's loud.

Art isn't cute.
It's brave.

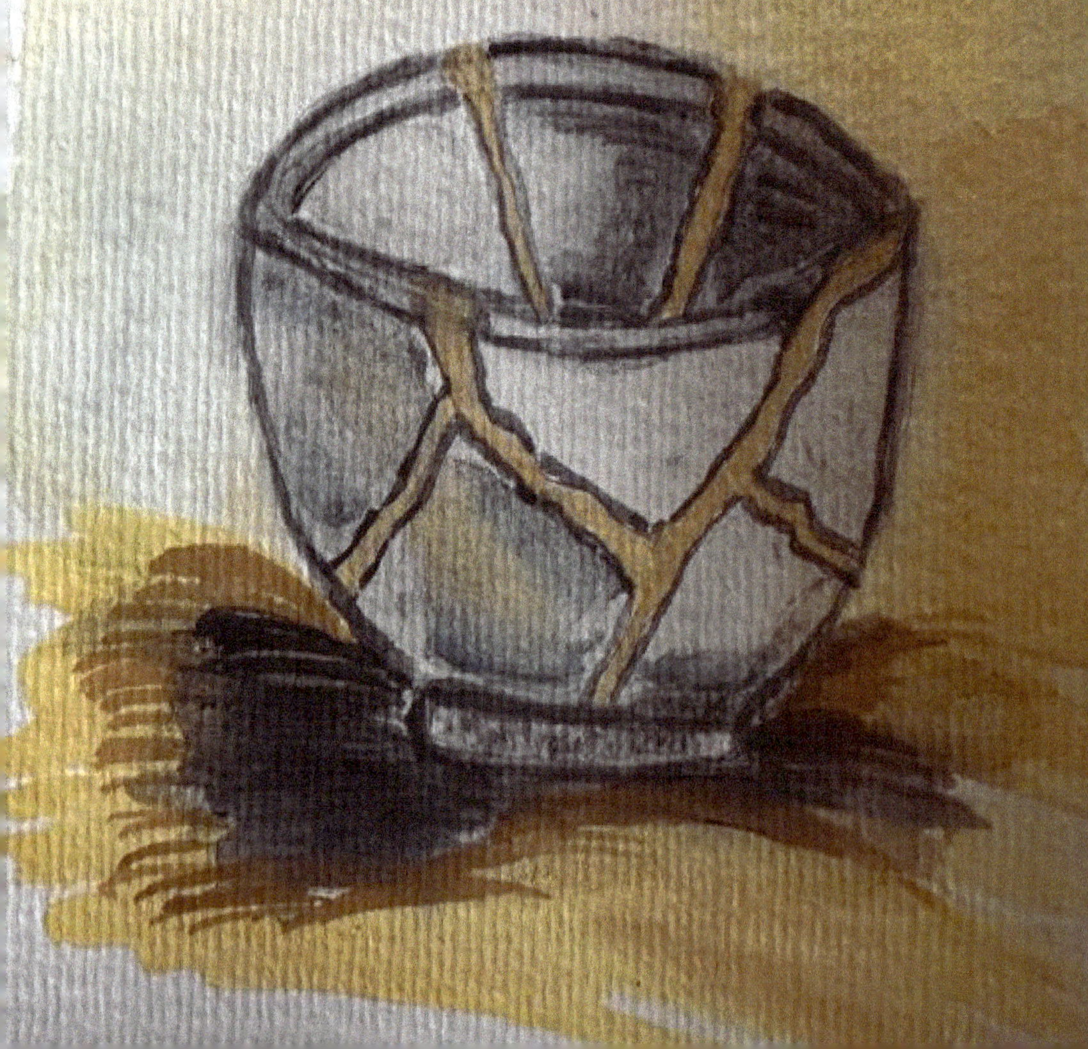

What Redefining Success Means to Me

Redefining success means realizing that:

- You don't have to follow a traditional path to be valid.
- Your version of a successful life might not look like anyone else's—and that's a good thing.
- Practice is more powerful than perfection.
- Fulfillment matters more than applause.

Success Requires Practice—Not Perfection

One thing I've learned—from my own work and from reading *The 7 Habits of Highly Effective People*—is that true success is built on habits. It's not a one-time win. It's a daily commitment.

- You show up.
- You do the work.
- You grow.

That's the secret. Not luck. Not talent. Not approval.

Just persistence.

And in the art world—or any world—that's what separates the dreamers from the doers.

Obstacles Will Happen. Let Them.

You will be misunderstood.

You will mess up.

You will feel behind.

But here's the difference:

People who redefine success keep going anyway.

Because life is a learning curve.

And every chapter—whether messy or magical—is part of the bigger masterpiece.

You Have to Believe, or at Least Try

I'm not saying it'll be easy.

But I am saying it's possible.

If you believe in what you're doing—or at least try to—if you give it enough time, heart, and consistency, success will find its way to you.

Maybe not in the way you imagined, but in the way you needed.

And that's the whole point of this book.

Final Thought

Success isn't fame.

Success isn't perfect.

Success is showing up, creating from your core, and redefining the finish line on your own terms.

So yes—keep creating anyway.

Because what you're building is worth it.

Part III:
The Life I Built

CHAPTER 7

FROM RANCH TO THE STUDIO

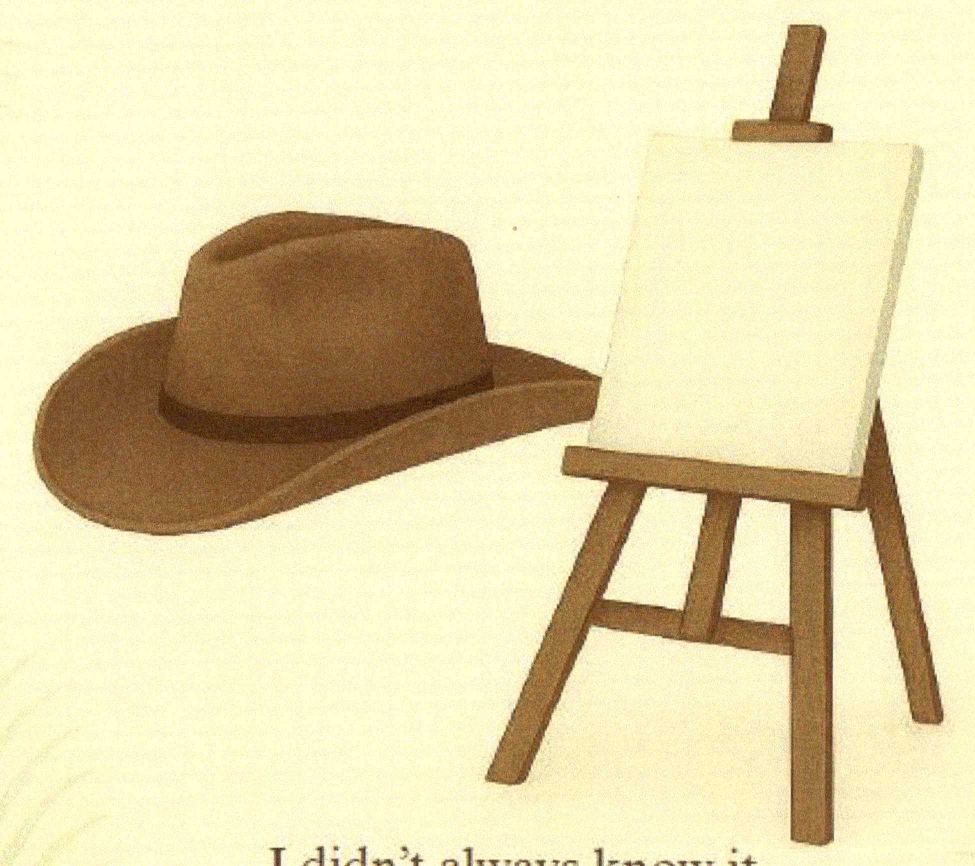

I didn't always know it would be my life – but looking back, I realized I built it piece by piece.

~

The quiet mornings feeding animals, the late nights holding a paintbrush, the camera strap slung over my shoulder at golden hour — all of it mattered.

My ranch in Wellington, Florida, isn't just land. It's a living, breathing space filled with imagination.

Those soft clucks of hens, the way my Charolais cattle move like poetry across the pasture, the rhythm of horse hooves, the ducks waddling to the pond, the gobble of turkeys in the background — they each have personality, a presence. They show up in my sketchbooks, in my paintings, in the colors I reach for when I don't even realize it.

It's because of them — and because of this place — that I opened my studio.

At first, it was small. A corner. A space where I could draw after chores were done. But over time, it grew into something more — a vision, a business, a lifestyle.

Someday, I hope it grows even bigger — into a full-time space where I can host **Paint & Sip** events under the stars, maybe right here on the ranch. Or maybe one day on a beach in the Bahamas. I dream of riding a horse down the shoreline in the morning and painting it by night. I imagine leading creative retreats, where I network with other artists, photograph vibrant sunsets, and let the brush tell the story.

And who knows — maybe someone would hang one of those paintings on their wall, and it would remind them to slow down too.

Art has a funny way of finding its people.

CHAPTER 8

MORNING ON THE FARM, NIGHTS IN THE STUDIO

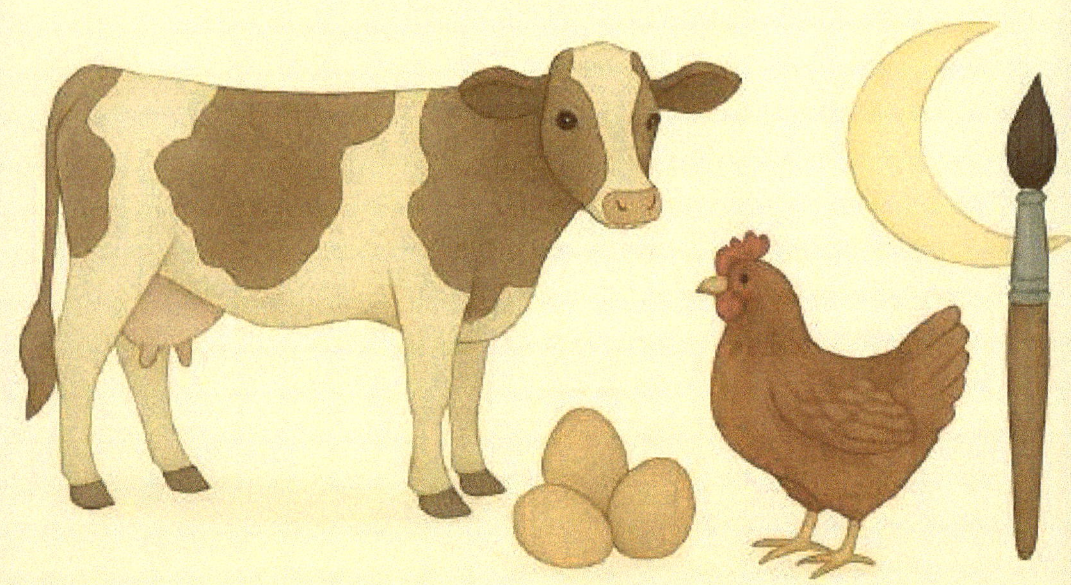

The work comes first. Always.

~

"Not all those who wander are lost." – J.R.R. Tolkien

Before the art, before the camera, before the studio lights turn on – I'm outside, boots in the dirt.

Mornings on the farm, feeding the cows, horses, mucking the stalls, checking the fences, making sure every animal is cared for. It's physical. It's gritty. It's humbling. But it's also grounding.

That kind of labor – the kind that makes your back ache a little and your hands rougher – is the kind that teaches you patience. And patience, I've learned, is a core ingredient in both farming and creating.

When the sun starts to set and the farm gets quiet, that's when the audio comes alive. Evenings are my favorite time to paint. There's something magical about the way the world settles down and your ideas rise up.

My art flows differently at night. The pace slows down. The brush moves with intention. And somehow, the work I did earlier in the day – the tending, the sweating, the listening – shapes the way I create.

This chapter in my life is all about balance: the work and wonder, the chores and the creation. It's a rhythm that's taught discipline, clarity, and how to listen to both the earth and my own voice.

It's also taught me that leadership doesn't come from being the loudest, most perfect – it comes from being consistent. Honest. Intentional.

And maybe, just maybe… all those early mornings and late-night painting sessions are preparing me for something bigger.

Which leads us right into what's next soon; a shift into the Heart & Mind of this journey, before we take a pause and reflect on a travel adventure.

Because when you work hard, lead with creativity, and stay grounded in your truth – who's to say you couldn't be president someday.

CHAPTER 9

EQUESTRIAN AT HEART

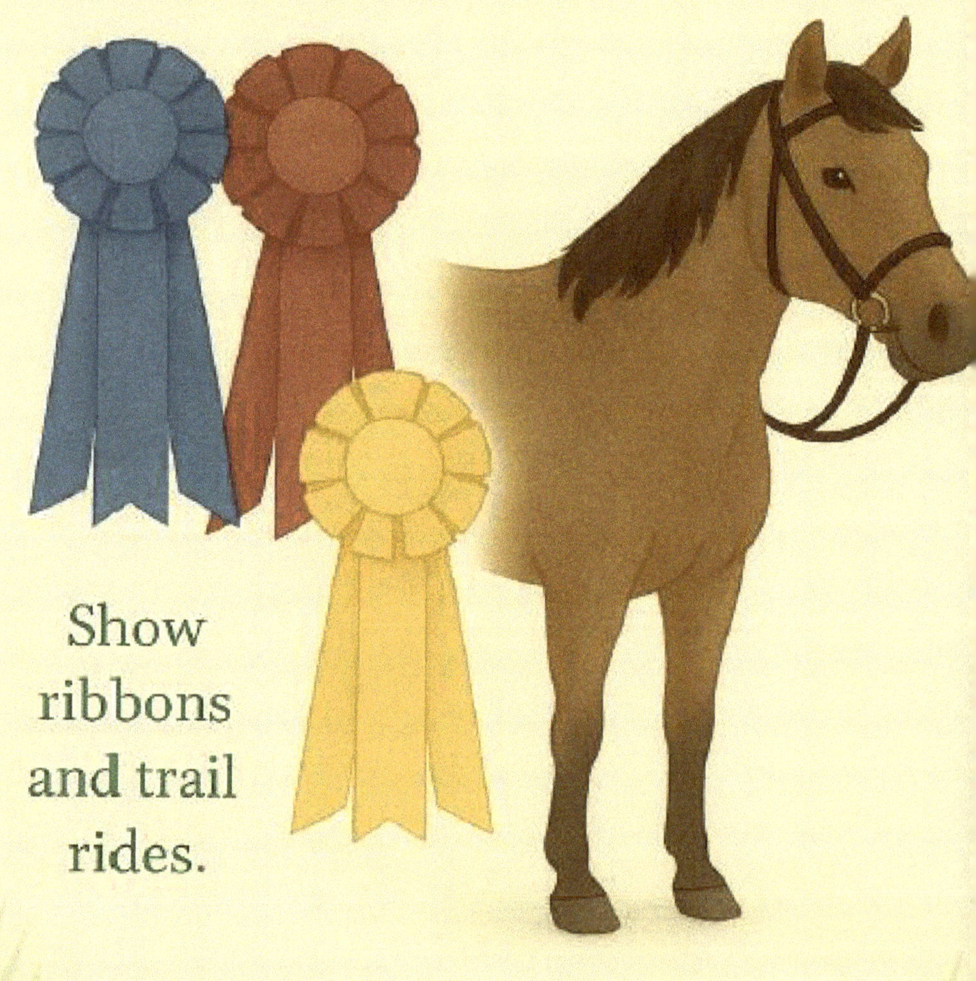

Show ribbons and trail rides.

~

I can't recall the exact moment I first loved horses, but I do remember the first one I loved.

Her name was Duchess.

A miniature pony who was, in horse years, nearly 100 and already blind when my grandfather—Poppy—brought her home. She had a nose for apples and carrots and a spirit far bigger than her size. My Poppy was one of the loudest men, but he was also steady. When he let me keep Duchess on the ranch and placed me on her back for the first time, it wasn't just a pony ride—it was a rite of passage.

I'd braid her mane, make up stories for us, and spend hours just sitting beside her. The quiet between us was sacred. That's where it all began.

As I grew older, horses became more than a hobby—they became my world. I spent summers at riding camps in North Carolina, learning to tack up, ride in both English and Western saddles, and hose down horses after dusty trail rides. We'd end the day around a stone pizza oven, smelling like sweat and hay, giggling with friends who felt like family.

I rode at day camps in Wellington, too—where we painted horses with our fingers, and I first realized my love for horses and my love for art weren't separate things. They could live in the same breath.

Then came Roxie—my first true show horse. I leased her from my trainer and rode nearly every day through middle and high school. She was calm and powerful, the kind of horse that made you feel brave just by being near her.

With Roxie, I competed in weekend shows, mucked stalls, polished boots, and learned what it meant to care for something completely. She taught me patience, presence, and poise.

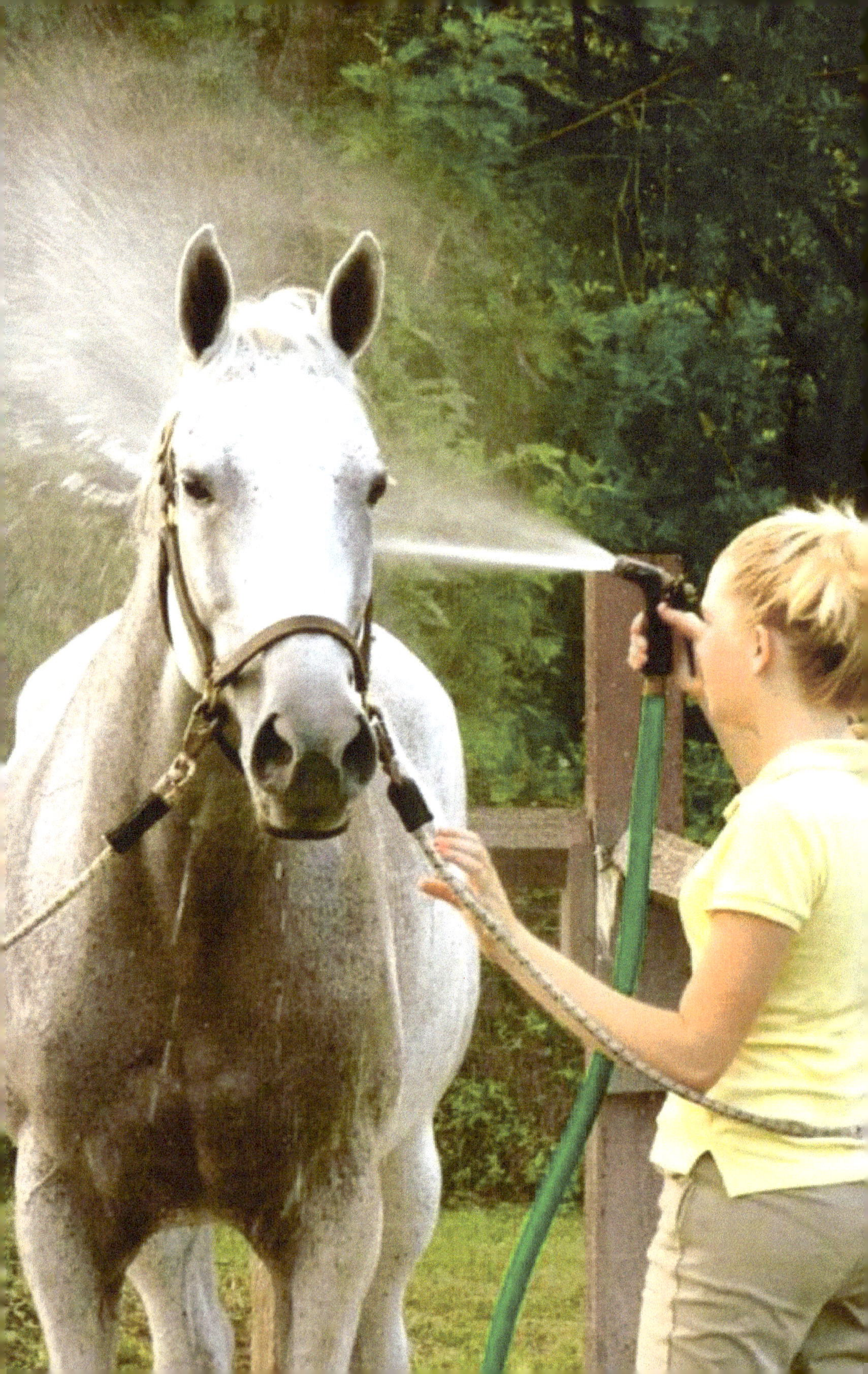

One summer, I attended the International Horse Camp in New York. This wasn't a camp with horses—it was a camp about horses. From dawn feedings to midnight barn checks, we lived the rhythm of the stable. It was discipline and wonder all in one.

I paused riding for a while—during the end of high school and into college—but in my final semester at Mississippi State, I signed up for an Intro to Horseback Riding class, just for fun.

The first time I swung into the saddle again, something clicked.

It brought me back to myself.

That ride—under the soft Mississippi sun—reminded me of everything I loved: horses, art, slowness, freedom, and the feeling that I was exactly where I was meant to be.

Now, horses remain at the center of my creative life. They are the subjects of my photographs, the lines of my sketches, and the rhythm in my stories. Through Nina Barr Studio, I get to honor them daily. I photograph horses across Wellington and beyond—at shows, in fields, during those quiet, unscripted moments that matter most. I draw them from memory and from life, trying to capture not just what they look like, but what they feel like.

Because when I pick up a pencil or look through my camera's viewfinder, I still feel like that girl in the barn aisle.

And I still hear Poppy's voice—calm and steady—saying:

"She's yours. Go on."

Because no matter where life takes me, I'll always be…

Equestrian at heart.

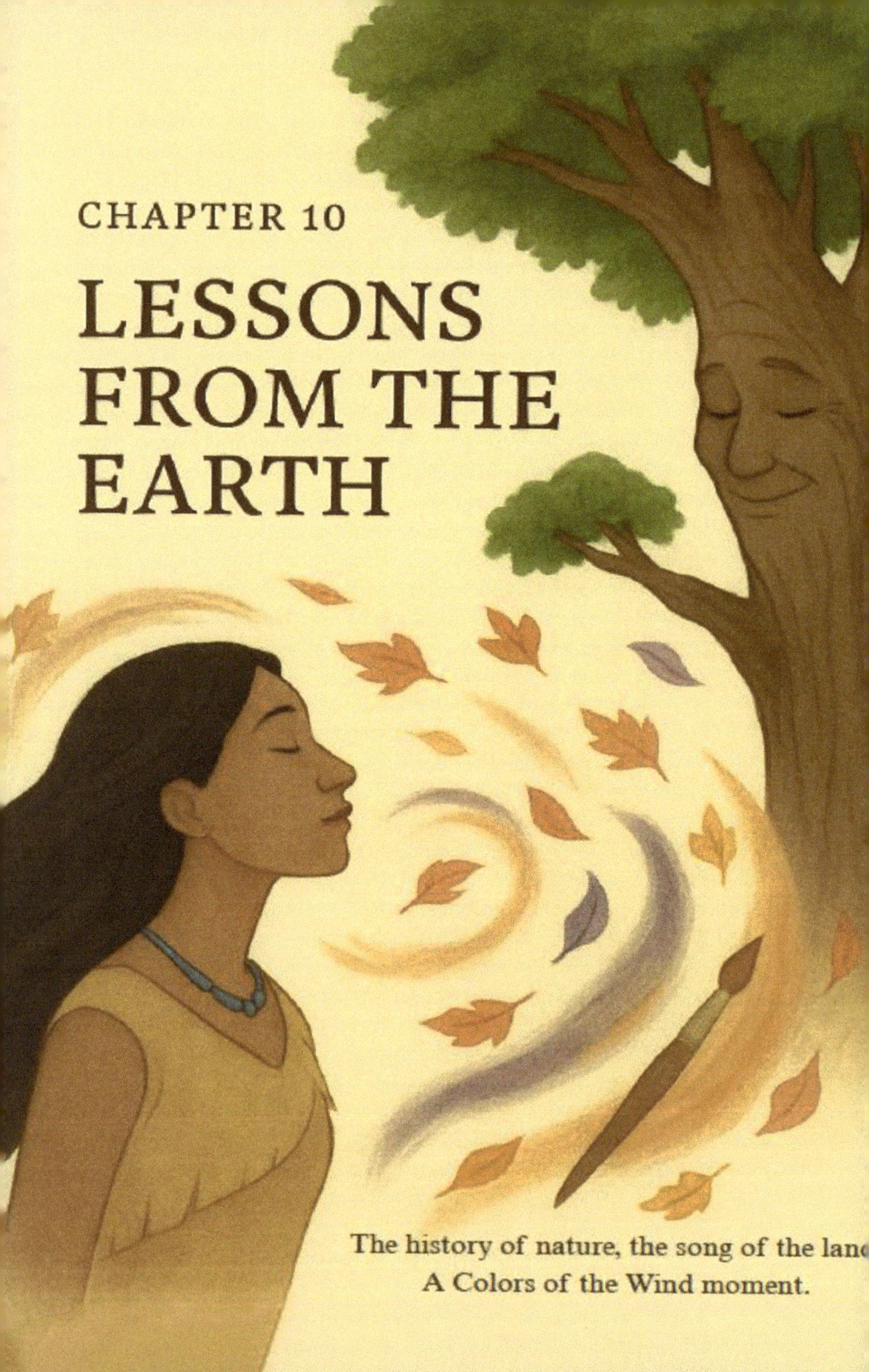
CHAPTER 10
LESSONS FROM THE EARTH
The history of nature, the song of the lan
A Colors of the Wind moment.

~

Nature is simply beautiful. But if we don't stop to look around, we'll miss it entirely.

We live in a world that rushes through red lights and scrolls past sunsets. A world where it's easy to forget that trees breathe, rivers sing, and wild horses still run free. But I haven't forgotten. I don't think you have either.

And if there's one animated voice that's always stayed with me – it's Pocahontas.

"You think I'm an ignorant savage…"

That line. That moment in *Colors of the Wind*, when Pocahontas speaks to John Smith – not with anger, but with a question. She asks him to see. To listen. To understand. She challenges him to walk the forest floor, to taste the berries, to paint with all the colors of the wind.

It wasn't just a Disney movie.

It was a lesson in empathy, in reverence, in nature.

A Brief Timeline of This Land

The history of the United States began long before we were even "the United States." Here's a simplified path that helps us remember the roots:

- 1607 – Jamestown, the first permanent English settlement.
- 1620 – The *Mayflower* lands; Pilgrims settle in Plymouth.
- 1776 – The Declaration of Independence is signed. We break from the British crown.
- 1789 – George Washington becomes the first President of the United States.
- 1800s–1900s – Expansion, war, reconstruction, civil rights, and beyond.

We weren't just building roads – we were building identity. A land filled with fields, flags, freedom, and flaws. But still – a land worth honoring.

Nature: the Greatest Artist of All

Why do I love art?

The colors.

The depth.

The mess.

The stories hidden in every brushstroke.

That's what nature offers us – every single day. A live painting. A perfect scene. A lesson in patience and change and growth. That's why I paint animals, oceans, and trees. Because they are alive with the truth.

And maybe that's why I feel so much when I hear the national anthem at a ballgame. Or when I see an eagle fly overhead. Or when the sun sets behind a pasture of Charolais cattle, and the wind carries just enough quiet to make you listen.

Sing the Song of the Land

In this fast-moving, often divided country, I think we need to come back to the basics.

Let kids climb trees again.

Let adults slow down enough to watch the birds.

Let us all sing the anthem – not out of duty, but out of love.

Because living in the USA is a song of the land.

And if you listen closely, it's humming all around you.

It sounds like rustling palms and Friday night lights.

Like horses galloping.

Like waves crashing.

Like freedom – and the responsibility that comes with it.

Final Thought

Maybe Pocahontas was right all along. You can't own the Earth. But you can learn from it. And if we listen – really listen – we'll hear stories whispered in wind, water, and the space between brushstrokes.

Before we can fix the world, we have to understand the ground beneath our feet. And that kind of understanding doesn't begin in a boardroom or political debate. It begins in the stillness. In the soil. In the soul.

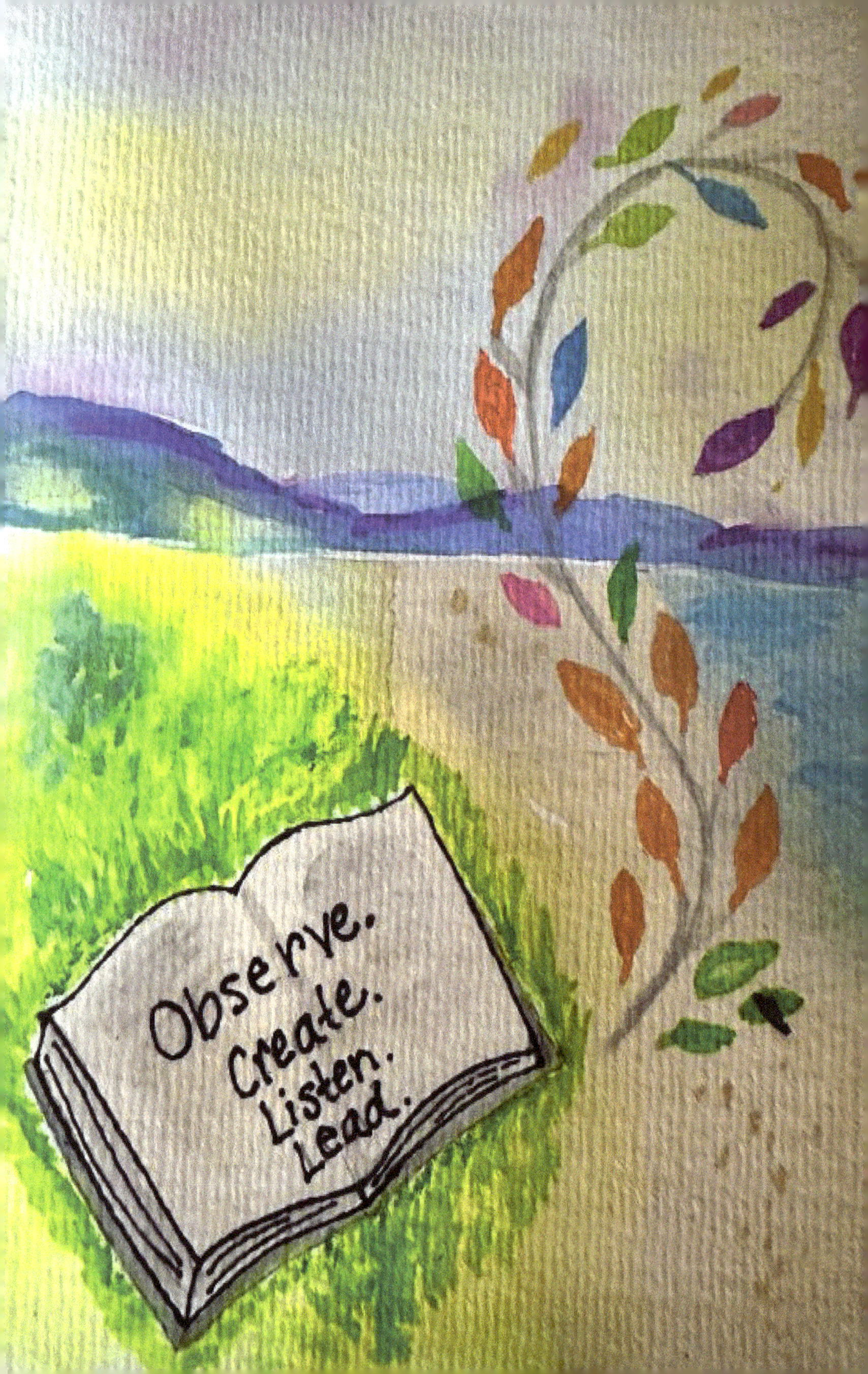
Observe.
Create.
Listen.
Lead.

For me, that stillness began where the Tennessee River curves around a town filled with front porches, chalkboards, and family stories – Florence, Alabama.

It's not just a place visited. It's where my imagination first learned to run wild – on docks and diving boards, barefoot in the backyard, or riding golf carts through the grass.

Just beyond the town, the Tennessee River widens into **Wilson Lake**, where our family's lake house rests on the shore. That house, that lake – it held a campfire, fishing lines, cousins laughing, and sunsets that practically painted themselves.

Before we travel the world or chase dreams across oceans, let's take a detour back. Back to where the river bends. Back to where the stories started.

"Listen with your heart, you will understand." – Pocahontas

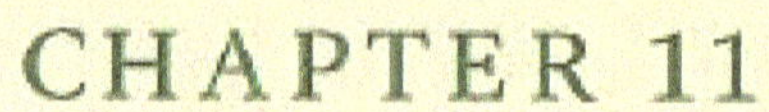

CHAPTER 11

WHERE THE RIVER BENDS

Florence, Alabama:

The Porch Where Art First Spoke to Me

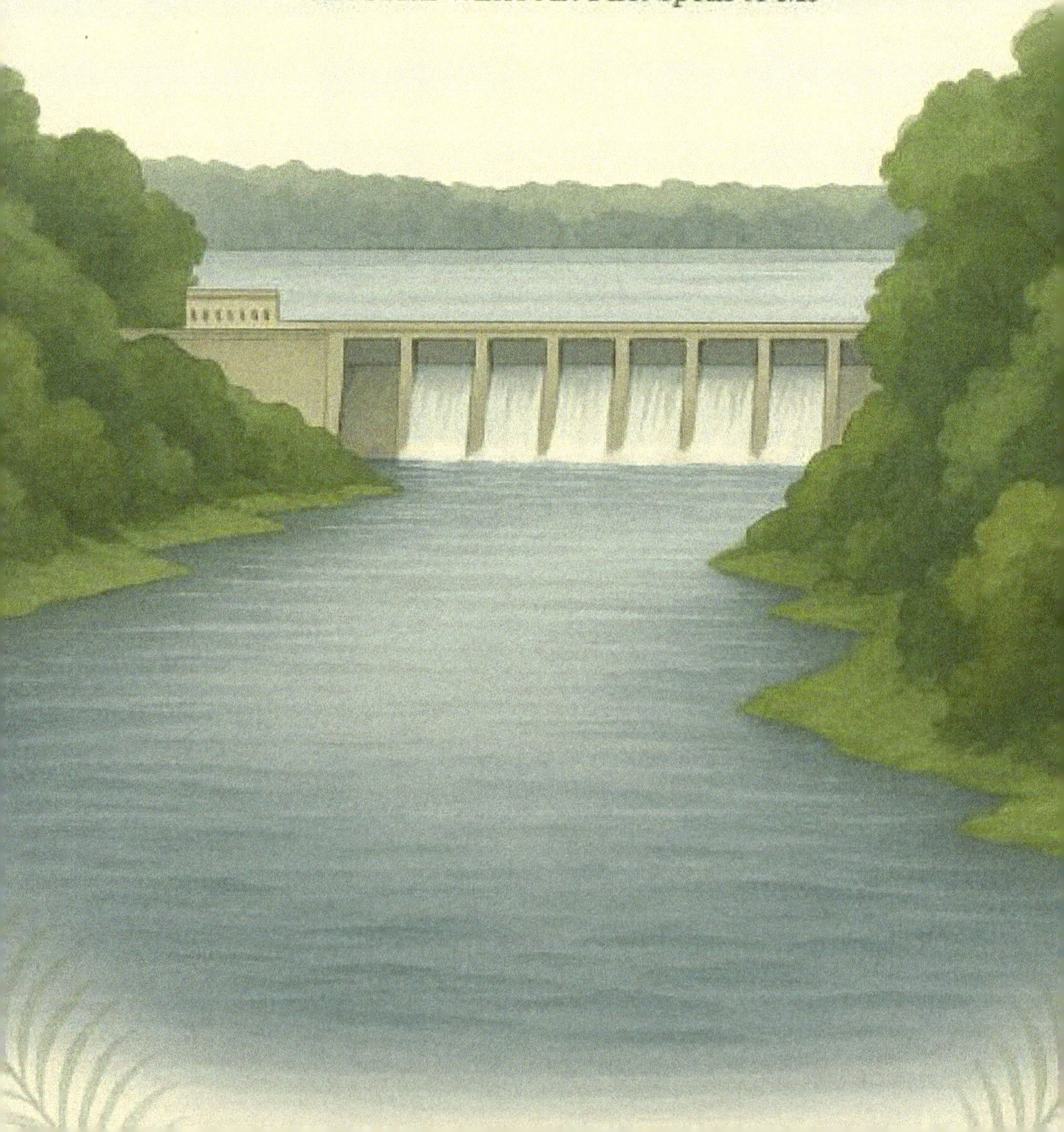

~

Before the beaches, before the horse shows, before the studio—there was Florence.

Not Florence, Italy, but Florence, Alabama. A small southern town that may not have been known for museums or marble statues, but it was my first gallery. My first classroom. My first quiet muse.

I remember sitting on the porch of our family's lake house, sketchbook in my lap, watching the sun slowly melt into the Tennessee River. Catfish rippled through the surface. Bass jumped when you least expected it. Breakfast was prepared every morning by my mother and aunts. The brushstrokes of sunrise and sunset were so real, so vibrant, I had no choice but to try and paint them.

At my grandmother and grandad's house, where my father grew up, there was an old chalkboard. Not for school—but for imagination. That's where I drew freely, with no judgment, just joy. Their house held stories, and somehow, that chalkboard helped me tell my own.

Downtown Florence had its own kind of magic. Brick buildings. Local bookstores. And then there was the University of North Alabama—where real lions live on campus. Not statues. Real lions. The mascot roars from a cage just steps away from classrooms. Even now, I can hear their echoes when I think of that town.

There were summers at Turtle Point Golf and Country Club, where I played golf and tennis, dove into the pool, and ate more plantation club sandwiches than I can count. Family dinners at local restaurants where the walls told as many stories as we did. Those days felt full—even when they were simple.

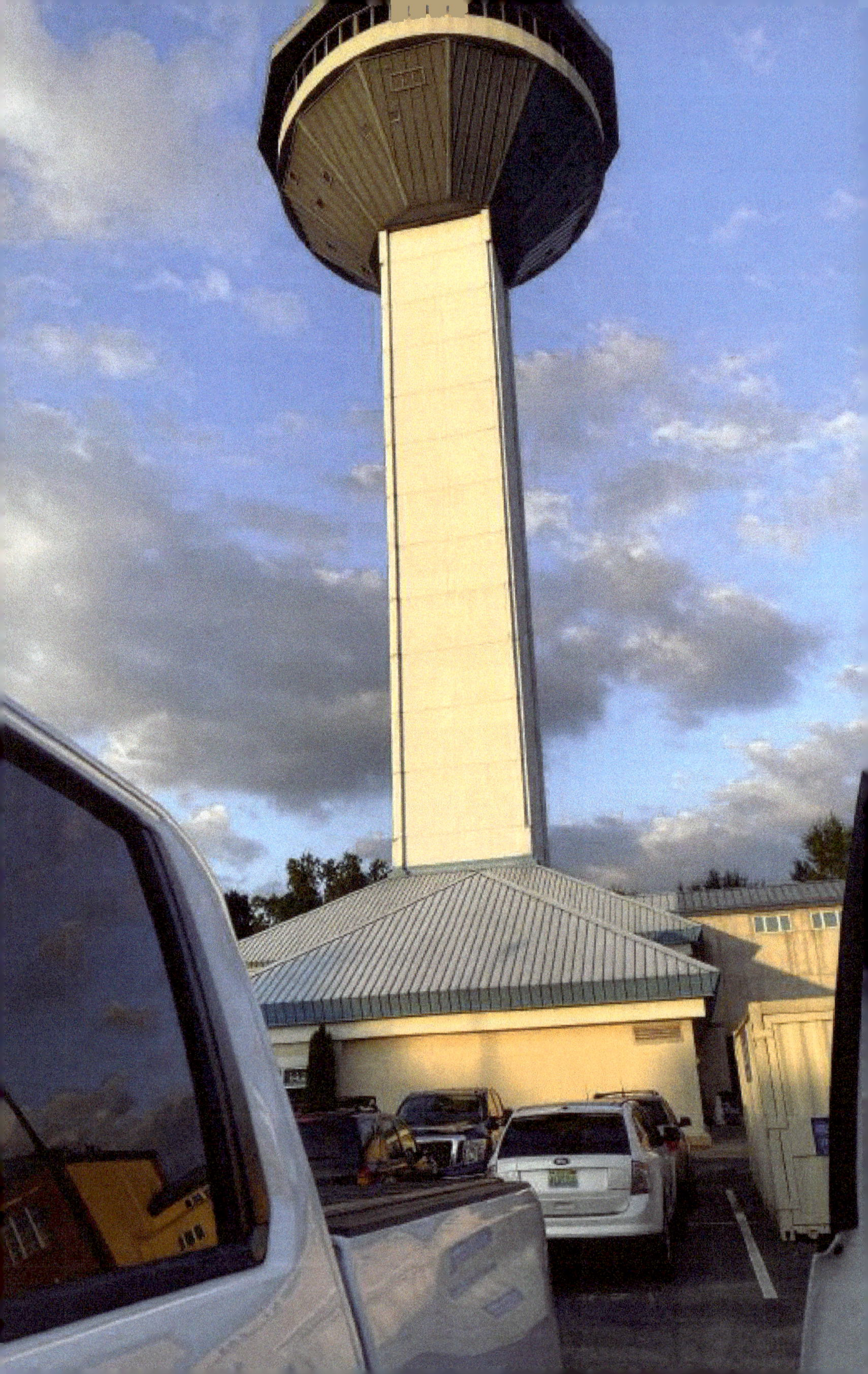

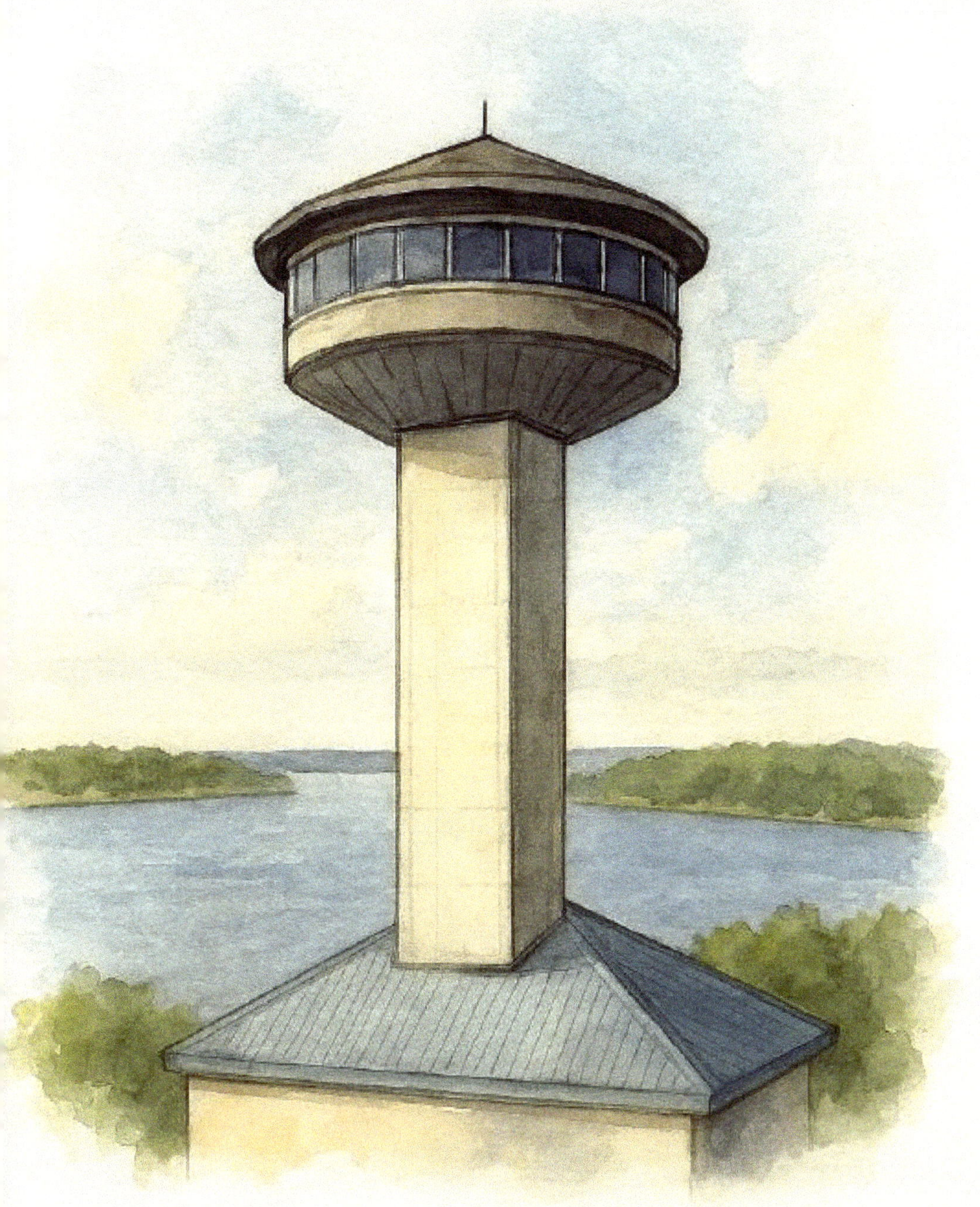

The kind of place where art
didn't need a frame.

360 Grille

The 360 Grille and Wilson Dam

One of those places was the 360 Grille—a restaurant perched above the river, slowly rotating with every passing minute. The view from up there was like stepping into a living painting: Lake Wilson shimmering below, the bridges stretched like ribbons over the water, and the Wilson Dam standing strong, holding history in its stones. Every time the floor turned, we saw another angle of home—sunlight on the bluffs, boats slicing the current, the silhouette of trees etched against the sky.

It was the kind of place where art didn't need a frame. The cocktails were elegant, the food rich, but it was the view that always stayed with me. A reminder that sometimes inspiration finds you in linen napkins and candlelight. That slow spin? It felt like the rhythm of Southern life. Steady. Observant. Grateful.

Before we'd head back down the elevator, we'd pause to take a look at the old photograph of Wilson Dam—black-and-white portraits of the men who built it, the early construction days, the engineering marvel it was meant to be. Completed in 1925, the dam helped power the region and shape the land, turning the floodplain into lake and legacy. It's more than a structure. It's a reminder of what's possible when you dare to shape your surroundings—an artist's instinct, too.

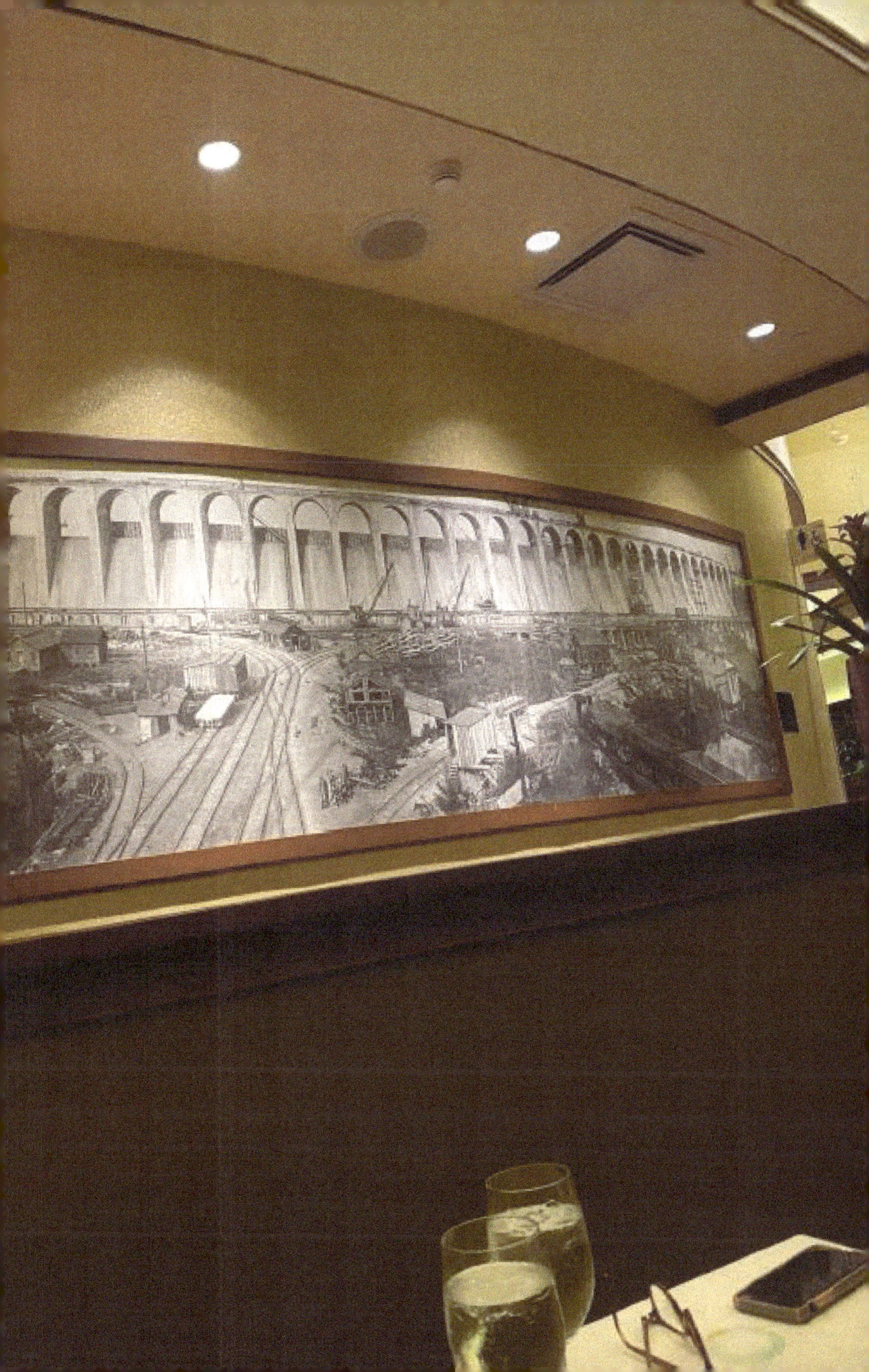

Maybe that's why we found ourselves drawn to the land beyond the water. On other days, we hiked the Natchez Trace, where the rocks and creeks whispered tales of centuries past. I remember picking blueberries at the neighbor's farm, running barefoot under the barn rafters, watching horses graze in the distance. The rock wall nearby—the one they say was built by hand during the "Trail of Tears"—felt sacred. I didn't know all the history back then, but I could feel it in the air.

And maybe that's why Pocahontas keeps showing up in my work. Maybe those early days in Alabama—the colors, the animals, the landscapes—were my first lessons in listening with my heart.

Florence taught me that art isn't something you do. It's something you live. It's Sunday afternoons on the porch. It's chalk dust on your fingertips. It's catfish swimming in golden hour light.

That little town shaped me.

And I've been sketching its echoes ever since.

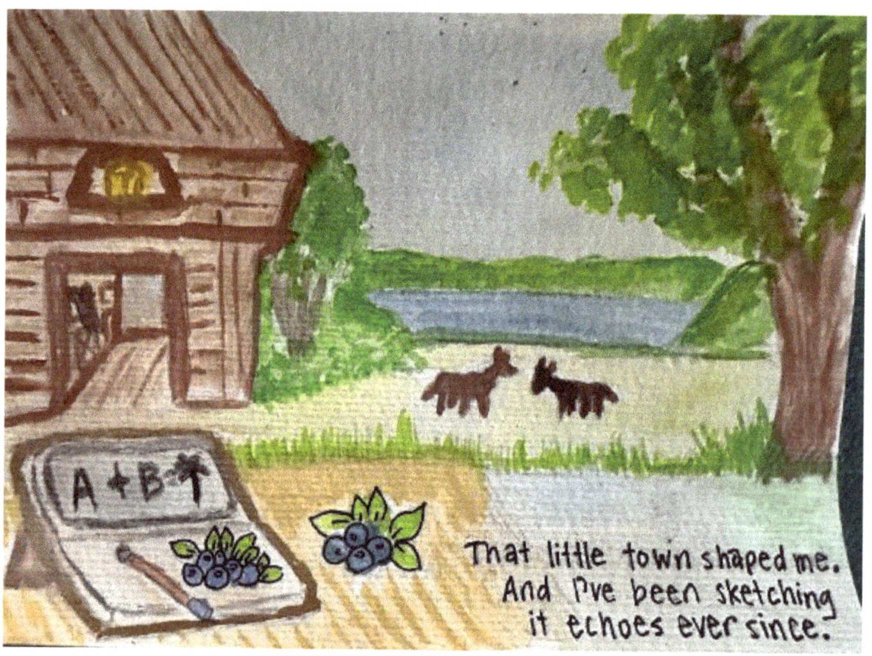

Florence wasn't just where we spent summers—it was where I first understood stillness. Where the imagination felt natural. Where I learned to see, to wonder, to remember.

Chalkboard sketch on the porch. Blueberries under the barn roof. Horse fields near the "Trail of Tears." It was all part of a slower, richer rhythm—one I still carry with me.

And then… the road opened up.

Sometimes growth doesn't happen in the hustle. It happens on the detours, the distance, the wide-open spaces between who we were and who we were becoming.

I began to travel more. To dream bigger. To see how air and life echo each other across the ocean, coast, and unfamiliar streets.

There's a whole world out there—and whether it's a muddy pasture or a rocky shoreline in Greece, each new place leaves a mark.

Let's wander a little further now.

And soon enough—we'll arrive at what matters most: the heart and the mind.

Exploring the entrepreneurial spirit and heritage of my American-British family.

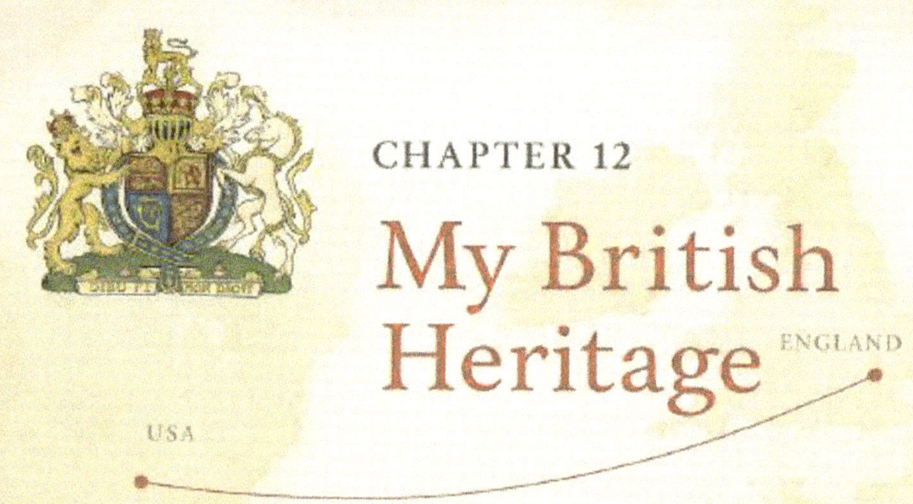

CHAPTER 12

My British Heritage

A tribute to the legacy I carry – across the ocean, generations, and the woman I was named after.

~

I've always been told I'm a little bit British. One-third, to be exact – and not just by blood. It was something my grandmother, **Nina Ling Barr**, reminded me of often.

"You're named after me, you know. Don't forget you've got England in you." She never let me forget it and honestly, I'm glad she didn't.

Nina was born in **Watford, Hertfordshire, England** in 1920 – a wartime child who became a wartime woman. She joined the fight against Germany in World War II, working in communications through the Battle of Britain. Her strength was quiet but unshakable – the kind of courage that didn't need to raise its voice to be heard.

After the war, she met my grandfather **Paul Edward Barr**, a pilot who flew 72 missions over Germany in a plane named *Black Magic*. He was a **Lieutenant Colonel** in the U.S Air Force and served in both **World War II and the Korean War**. After the war, he studied architecture at Auburn University and Nina followed him to America, where they built their life in **Florence, Alabama.**

He went on to design churches. Buildings, and community spaces throughout the region – and I like to think that's where I get my artistic gene from. His lines became walls, steeples, and homes. My lines became brushstrokes, photos, and stories. In different ways, we both made a living out of vision.

They lived in the same house on Decatur Avenue for decades – the same house where my father grew up, and the same one I would return to every summer on the Fourth of July. There, surrounded by driftwood, paintbrushes, jet skis, family dinners, and legacy, I found a second kind of home – not just in place, but in people.

Nina was so much more than a grandmother. She was the glue, the grace, the quiet force. And sometimes, not so quiet. She had a voice – sharp, witty, and just a little loud – like my grandfather, Poppy.

She loved golf. And she watched it religiously – always cheering for Phil Mickelson, always raising an eyebrow at Tiger Woods, never in a harsh way. Just her own version of loyalty – and a little playful stubbornness, too. If Phil was on, don't even try to change the channel.

And if the topic of England ever came up, you better believe she'd break into "Rule, Britannia!" with that unforgettable twinkle in her voice:

"Rule, Britannia! Britannia rules the waves..
Britons never, never, never, never shall be slaves!"

She sang it proudly. She taught it to us like it was history and identity in one. And it kind of was.

She volunteered for the Salvation Army. She led women's groups, supported the arts, and served as a Sunday school teacher at Trinity Episcopal Church. She loved bridge, garden clubs, tennis, and Auburn football – maybe more than anyone should.

But most of all, she loved her family and she loved this country – even though she never forgot the one she came from.

I am her namesake,

I am her grandchild.

And I am – proudly, deeply – a piece of her story.

She would be proud to see her name printed here. And I hope she knows – she helped write mine.

"Legacy isn't about faith or inheritance. It's about memory, meaning, and the way someone's spirit shows up in the way you live your life. Nina Ling Barr – this chapter is yours"

And I can still see her there — sitting on the back porch of the lake house, cup of English tea in hand, a Krispy Kreme donut by her side, and hummingbirds dancing at the feeders around her. That was her favorite view. Her peace. Her routine. She brought the donuts when she drove up from Decatur Avenue, like clockwork. And when she'd settle into her chair, smile soft and eyes lifted to the trees, it was like the world slowed down just for her.

That's how I remember her: steady, sweet, a little sharp — and always surrounded by beauty.

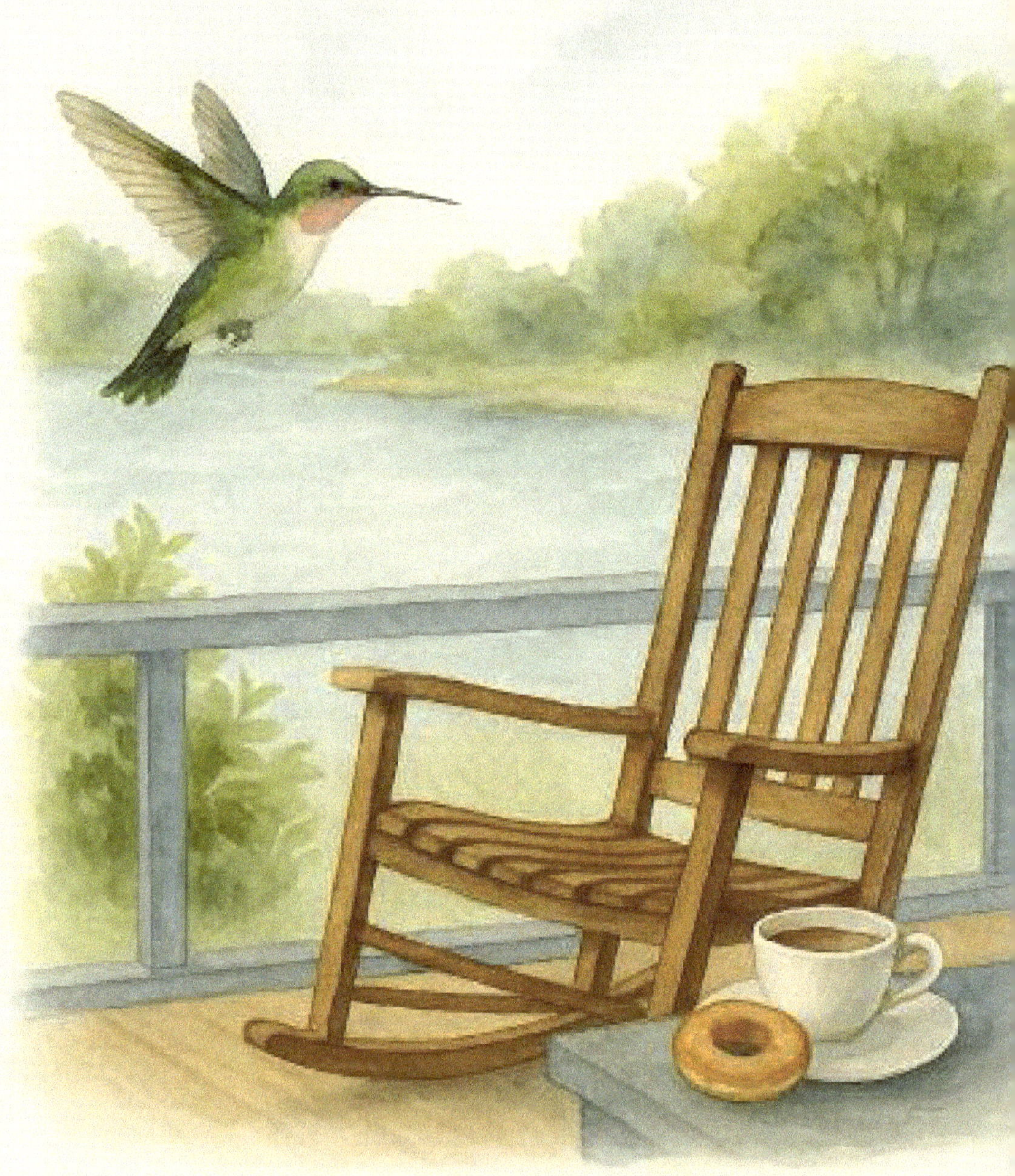

And I can still see her there—sitting on the back porch of the lake house, cup of English tea in hand, a Krispy Kreme donut by her side and hummingbirds dancing at the feeders around her.

That's how I remember her: steady, sweet, a little sharp—and always surrounded by beauty.

CHAPTER 13

The Gustafson and Otto Family Legacy

LEGACY LINES

THE ONES WHO BUILT BEFORE ME

How the American dream shaped mine.

~

If the British side of my family taught me about elegance and resilience, the American side taught me about grit, work ethic, and how to make something out of nothing. They were builders. Dreamers. Entrepreneurs with their sleeves rolled up.

My mother's side of the family – the Gustafson and Ottos – were a little bit of everything: German, Swedish, Pennsylvanian, New Jersey-born, and deeply South Florida-rooted. You could say we were a mix. A beautiful mutt of culture and stories – and all of them left a mark on me.

Patricia Carol Otto Gustafson: My grandmother aka "MooMaw" – born on **Christmas Eve in 1919**, in Philadelphia. She lived through the Great Depression, WWII, and raised a close-knit family alongside her husband, **Tom Gustafson**, for more than 50 years.

"She was the wind beneath his wings," as he always said – and he meant it.

A quiet powerhouse. They ran **Tom Gustafson Industries**, a painting and roofing company that became legendary in South Florida – known for its catch jingle, "*TOM GUSTAFSON!*" and the iconic slogan "Snow White Roofs."

Together, they raised five children – including my mother – and ran businesses. Little League teams and community circles like it was all second nature. My grandfather even became known throughout Florida thanks to his son, Tom Jr. who went on to serve as **Speaker of the Florida House of Representatives** in 1988.

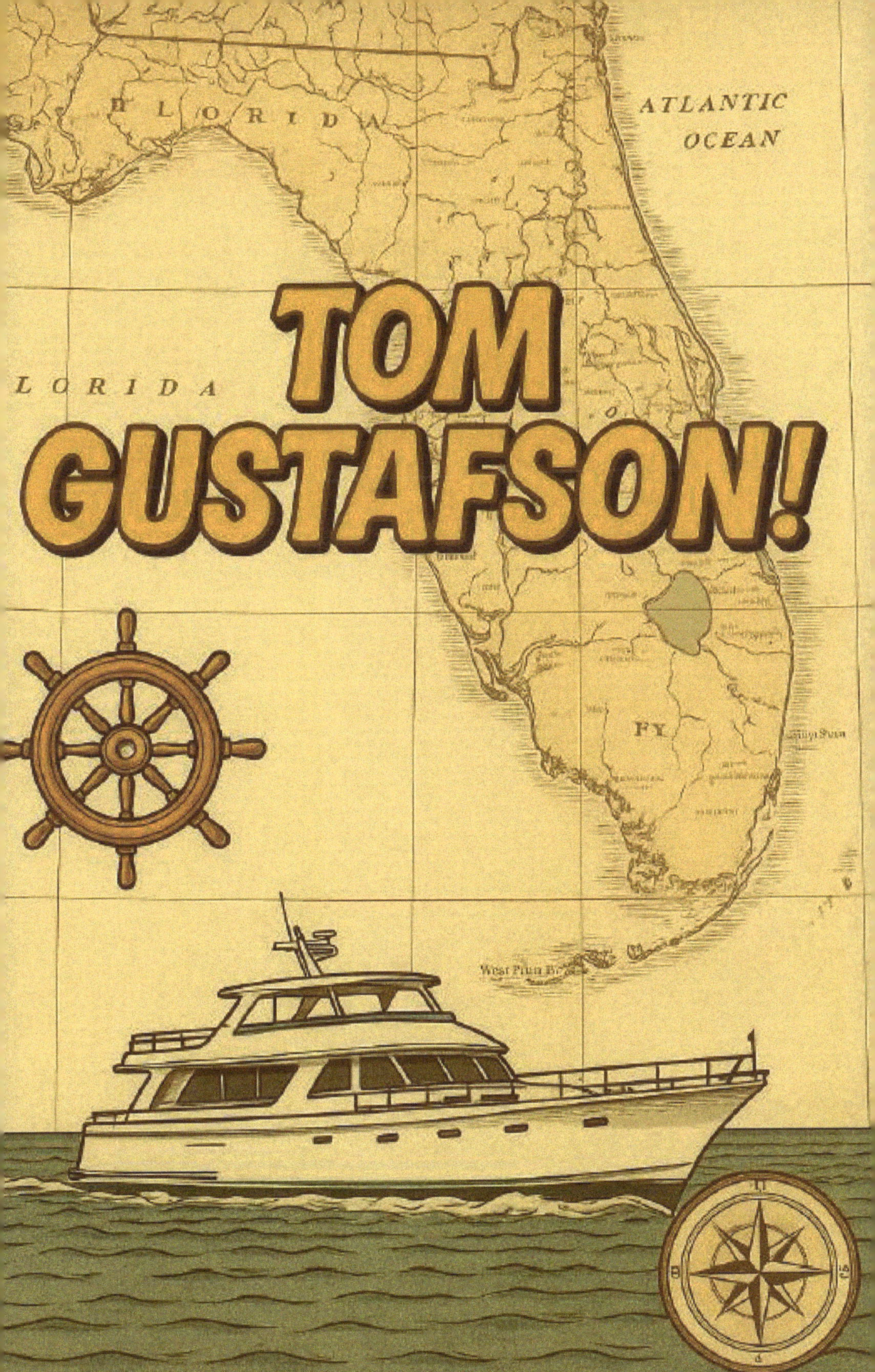
ATLANTIC
OCEAN
LORIDA
TOM
GUSTAFSON!

Sunshine, Salt, and "One More Time"

But Poppy wasn't just about business. He loved the water. And our family lived for it.

At any given time he was either leasing or captaining a yacht – often under the name **One More Time**. He was always planning the next fishing, afternoon cruise, or boat day with his children and friends.

We all were raised around **boats, sunshine, fishing poles, and sunscreen in our hair**. Some families gathered around a dinner table – we gathered around the dock. Some passed down heirlooms – we passed down **anchors, outboards, and stories about the sea.**

Because let's be honest – we're rooted in **South Florida**. The salt air is practically in our DNA.

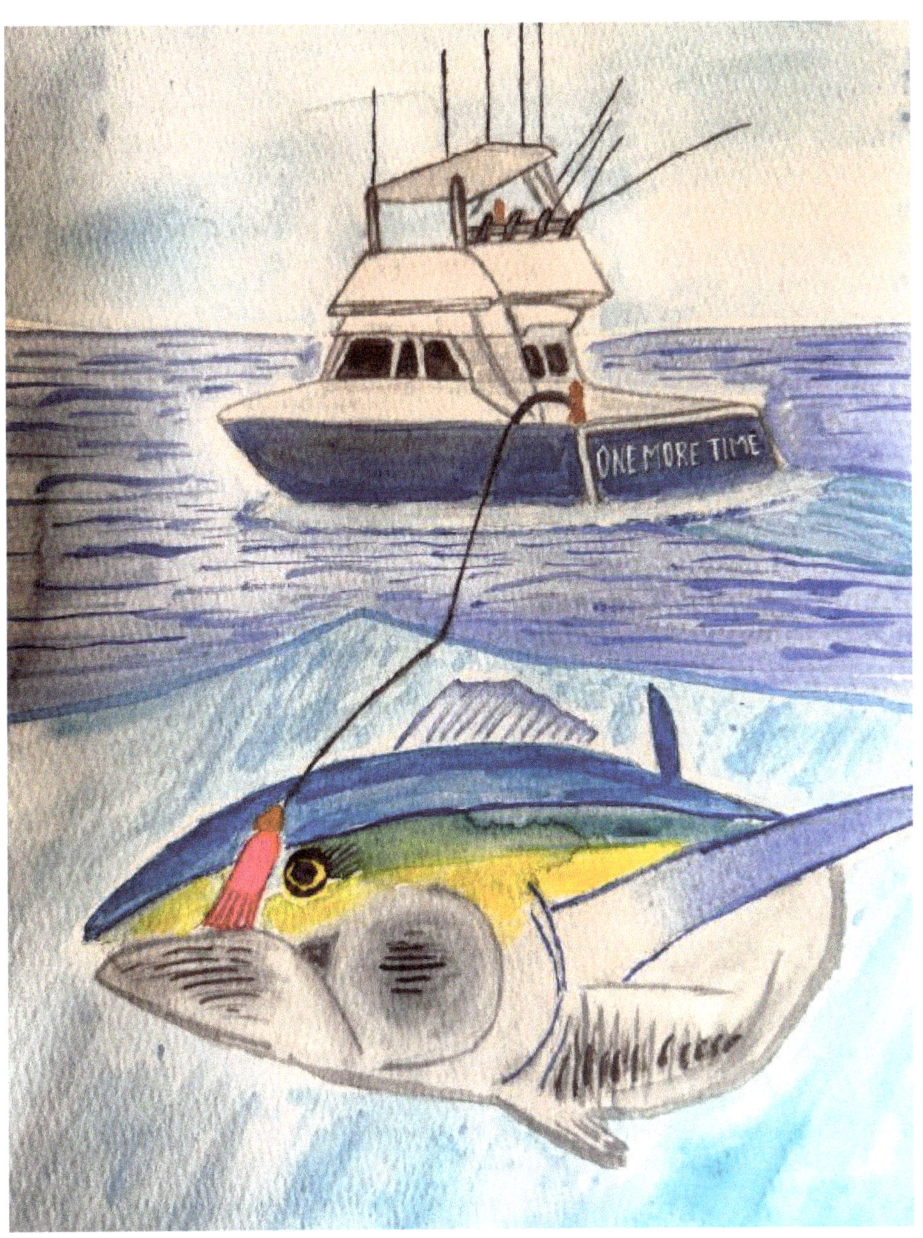

Watercolor and sketch by Nina Barr

A Legacy of Doing the Work

They weren't glamorous. They were **gritty**. They weren't always soft-spoken. But they were loyal.

They weren't royalty — but they were **family legends** in their own right.

They were the kind of people who built businesses from scratch and expected their grandkids to **graduate college** – because anything less wasn't an option.

From **Fort Lauderdale to Ocean City, New Jersey,** from **boardwalks to rooftops**, this side of my family taught me about sea, service, and showing up with pride.

I may carry the name Nina from my British grandmother, but I carry my **work ethic, hustle, and heart** for the Gustafson and Ottos.

And I carry a deep love for saltwater days and "one more time" boat rides – from **Poppy**.

They were a little loud. A little stubborn, but always present. Always building. Always proud. And I'm proud to be one of them.

They taught me how to build something real. But the next part of the story? It's about where I

learned to let go, explore, and follow whatever road called my name.

Part IV:
Wide Open Spaces

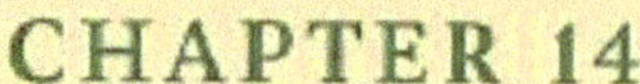

CHAPTER 14

POSTCARDS FROM THE ROAD

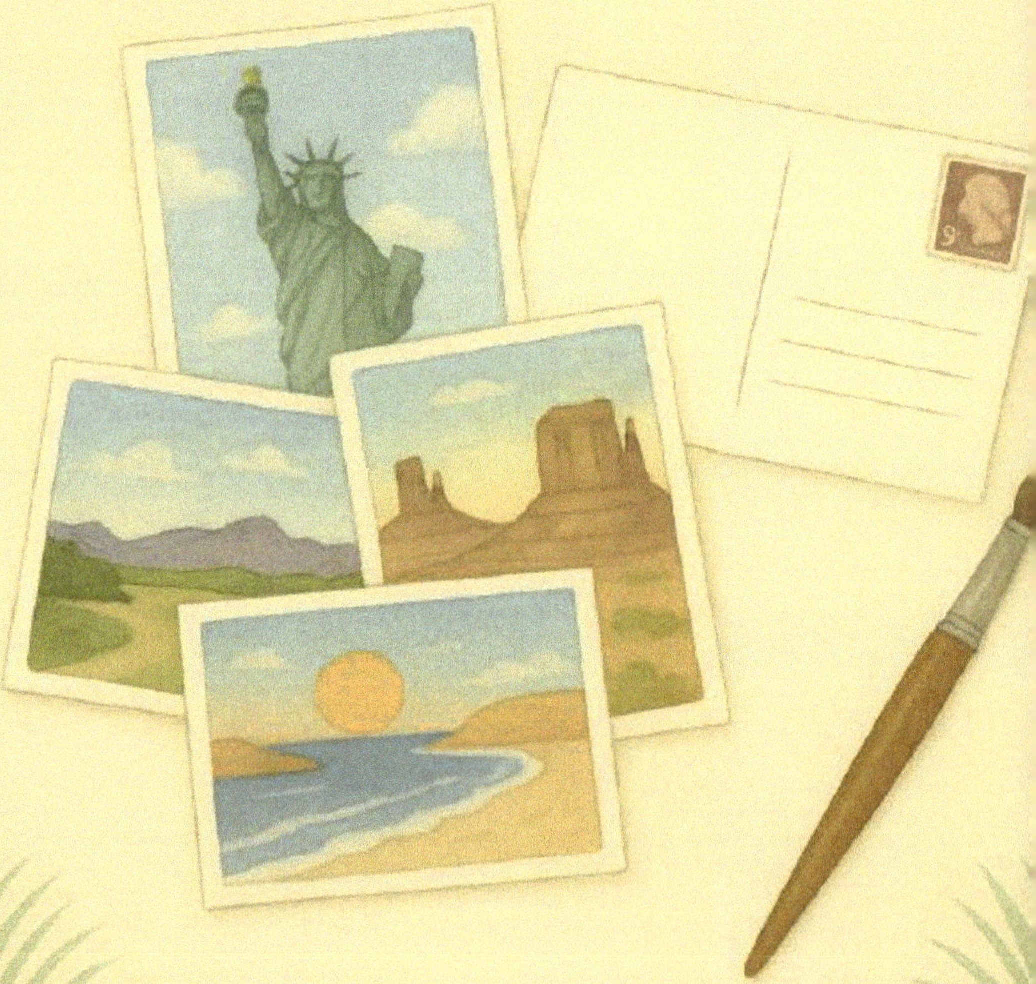

From building from scratch to building a life worth wandering through.

~

There's something sacred about taking a break—about pausing long enough to look around and realize,

"I built this life."

After the hustle, the pressure, and the long nights spent drawing, editing, and hoping—it's okay to slow down and breathe.

That's what this chapter is about: the moments in between the work. The travels. The quiet resets.

And yes—some really good road trip playlists.

You Don't Have to Go Far

Not every trip has to be a passport stamp.

Sometimes, it's as simple as packing a beach towel, grabbing the dogs, and driving down to the coast.

Those are some of my favorite days.

No pressure, no itinerary. Just the Florida breeze, soft light, and the feeling that time has slowed down.

But I also believe in big adventures.

The World I've Wandered

I've been lucky enough to travel, even when I didn't realize I was collecting inspiration.

As a teenager, I explored France—from the lavender fields of Provence and the museums of Paris to the glitz of Monte Carlo. I fell in love with everything from fresh crepes to fine art.

Costa Rica, Belize, The Bahamas, and Cozumel followed—each place painting its own colors into my memory. The warm sun, the bright boats, the rhythm of new cities… all of it finds its way back into my art.

One day, I imagine being there again—maybe for a Longines equestrian show or to hang a piece in a French gallery under my name: *Nina Barr Studio – Paris Edition.*

A girl can dream, right?

Where I Want to Go Next

I've got a bucket list just like anyone else.

At the top?

- Italy – for the art, the olives, the light.
- Japan – for the structure, the contrast, the cherry blossoms.
- Maine – yes, Maine. For the cliffs, the lighthouses, and the slow coastal mornings.

Maybe I'll write a photography book.

Maybe I'll make a coloring book inspired by the seas, markets, and mountain roads.

Or maybe I'll just keep collecting memories and turning them into art.

Why Artists Need to Leave Home Sometimes

There's something about seeing another part of the world that shakes your routine loose.

You see new colors. Hear new sounds. Taste new palettes. And in that shift—you find new parts of yourself.

That's the power of travel.

It's not about escape.

It's about expansion.

Professional Possibilities, Too

For artists and photographers, travel isn't just personal—it's professional.

There are artist residencies abroad, photography tours, and even curated retreats like VAWAA (Vacation With an Artist), where you can learn from master craftsmen in their own studios.

There are shows in Europe, markets in South America, galleries in cities you haven't even discovered yet.

And every time you step into a new place, you bring your story—and your camera—with you.

Final Thought

My dream?

That *Nina Barr Studio* becomes something more than a local name.

That it travels with me—through brushstrokes, prints, and photographs shared around the world.

I've been lucky to see some incredible places already—from the streets of Paris to the beach of Belize. But something tells me the best journeys are still ahead.

And now, I can't help but ask myself… **Where should I go next?**

CHAPTER 15

WHERE SHOULD I GO NEXT?

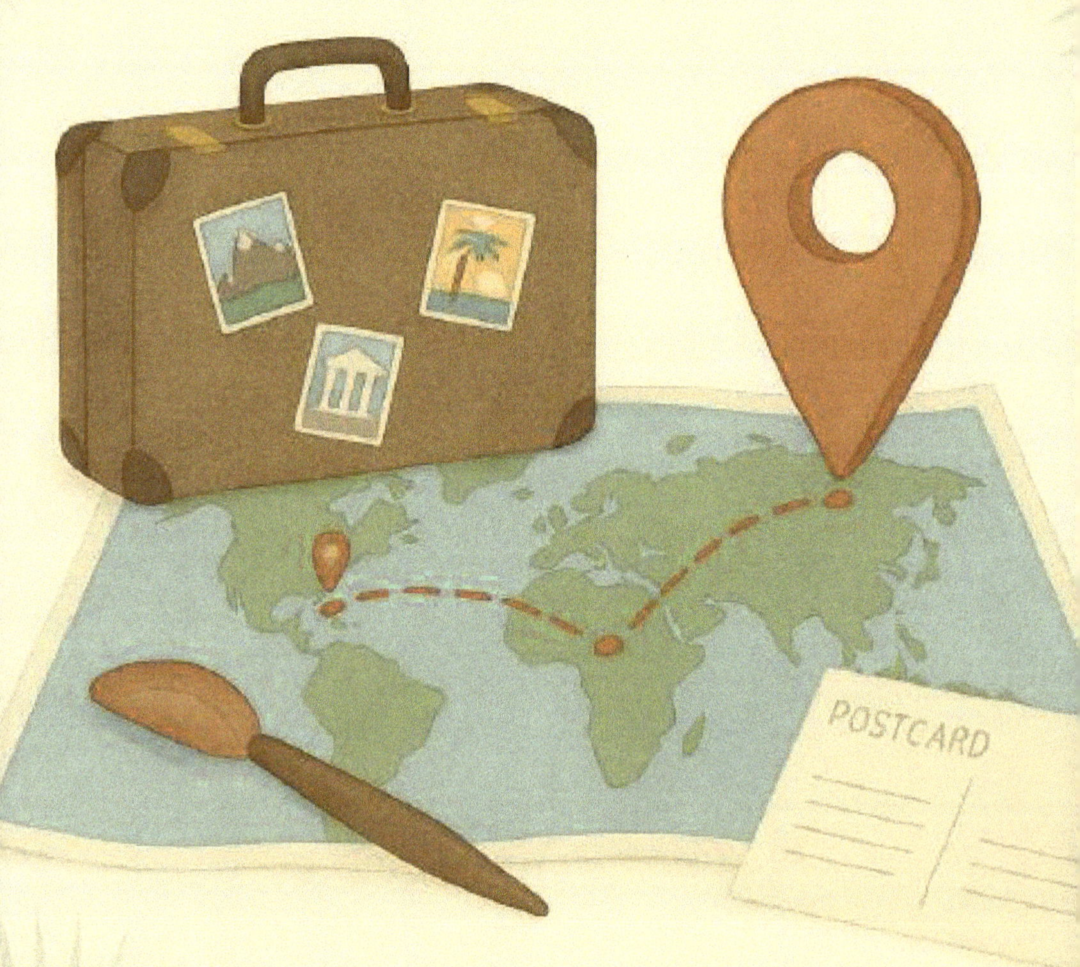

A wandering heart's bucket list – with art and animals in mind.

~

Some people make bucket lists in journals. Others scribble them in the margins of calendars or dreams. Mine has always lived in my head – between brushstrokes and camera clicks. After years of building, creating, and slowly stepping into this life as an artist, I've started wondering more and more:

Where do I go next?

It's Not Just Travel – It's Creative Expansion

For me, travel isn't just a vacation. It's inspiration. It's a reset. It's how I fill my soul with new textures, colors, and emotions that eventually spill back out onto canvas or paper or screen.

Whether I'm walking through a small coastal town with my camera or sketching from a quiet ranch porch, the world has a way of offering new perspectives – if you're willing to see them.

My Artistic Bucket List

Here are the places tugging at my heart right now – each one promising a different kind of creative magic:

- **Italy** – For its sun-drenched landscapes, ancient cities, Renaissance art, and Lipizzaner horses.
- **Japan** – For its intentional beauty, cherry blossom season, minimalism, and structure.
- **Maine** – For rugged coastlines, quiet lighthouses, moody harbors, and foggy mornings.
- **Iceland** – For wild horses, volcanic terrain, Northern Lights, and wide-open spaces.
- **Spain** – For flamenco energy, equestrian heritage, and vibrant color palettes.
- **Scotland** – For Highland cows, Loch Ness monsters, castles, and misty green hills.

- **Argentina** – For the vast pampas, gaucho culture, and untouched countryside.

Studio Dreams on the Move

One day, I'd love to host a pop-up gallery show in a city I've never lived in. Or lead a travel art workshop in a tucked-away coastal town. Or spend two weeks learning from a printmaker in Japan through something like VAWAA – Vacation With an Artist.

I want to create everywhere – not just in Florida or my studio, but in the rhythm of new places. Maybe even write an art book about it. Or publish a travel-inspired coloring book for fellow wanderers and makers.

Who knows? Maybe Nina Barr Studio becomes both a home base and a passport stamp.

Art, Animals & Adventure

If there's one theme that runs through all these destinations – it's this:

I want to be surrounded by animals and art wherever I go.

I want to ride horses in new landscapes.

I want to sketch cattle in countryside pastures.

I want to paint ocean views from cliffs I've never stood on before.

I want to feel a place deeply enough to recreate it through color and story.

A Final Thought

This chapter isn't just a list of places I hope to see. It's a reminder that even if I've built something beautiful already, there's still more to explore.

So I'll keep creating. Keep packing a camera. Keep letting curiosity lead the way.

Because I don't want to live the same year on repeat. I want my work – and my life – to be a collection of **postcards and possibilities.**

Now the other question is… **Where should I go next?**

Now that we've dreamed, let's return home.

To what stirs the soul.

To the big questions.

To the fire inside.

Welcome to **Part V: Heart + Mind.**

Part V:
Heart & Mind

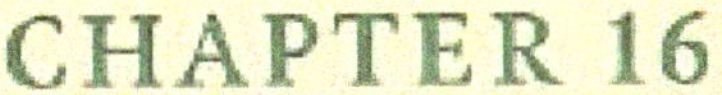

CHAPTER 16

A WORLD IN MOTION

Politics, war, and staying sensitive in a world that often isn't

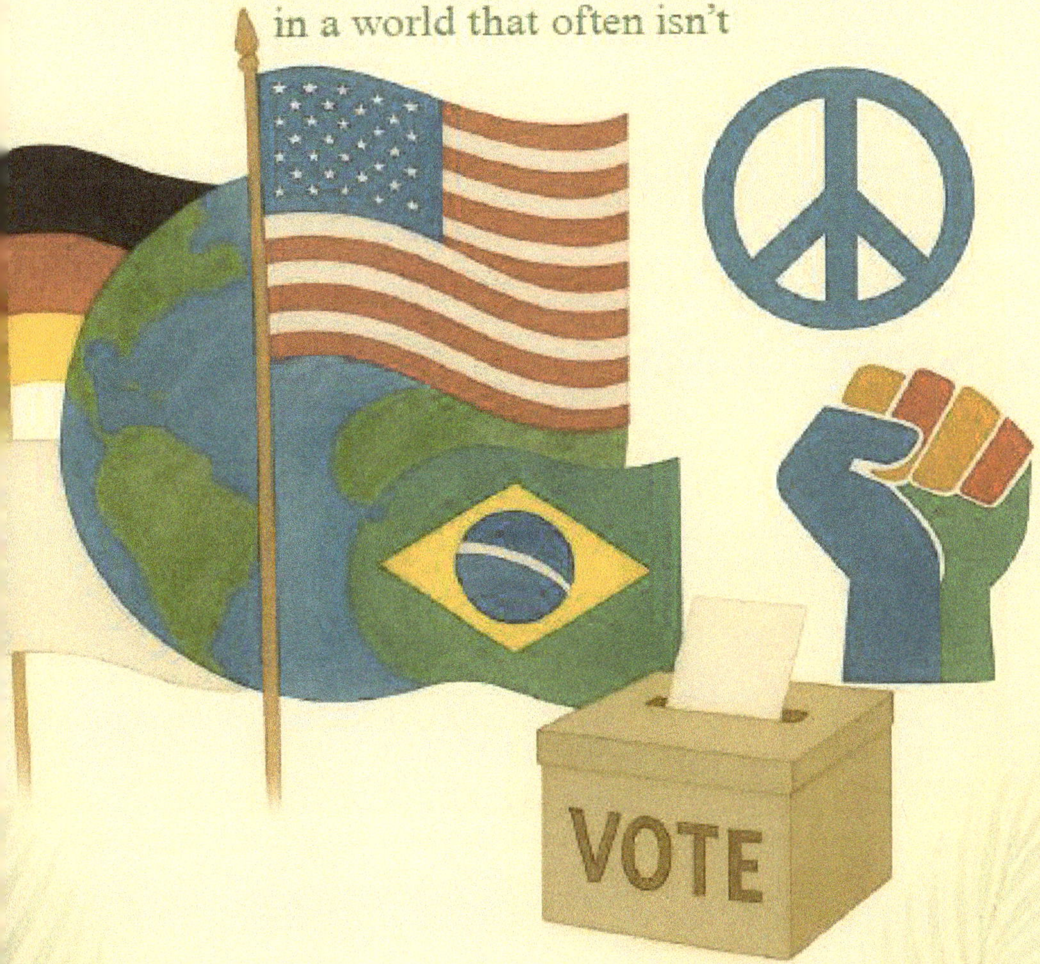

~

When I first registered to vote, I didn't fully understand the weight of political identity. I was 16, applying for my driver's permit when the DMV clerk casually asked what party I wanted to be in when I turned 18. It felt like I had to pick a team before I even knew the rules of the game.

Over time, I became more grounded in my views. I'm a white female conservative. I lean Republican—not because I hate the other side, but because I believe in structure, values, and the ability of the individual to work hard and build something meaningful. I believe in land, tradition, freedom, and faith. I also believe you can be compassionate and conservative. Those two are not opposites.

I grew up with cattle, crops, horses, and hard work. I believe in preserving farmland, honoring our country's roots, and keeping the American dream alive—not through division, but through grace. Not by yelling, but by creating. Maybe that's why this chapter belongs in a book called *Keep Creating Anyway*.

The Trump Era & Beyond

The Trump years stirred the pot—no denying that. He was bold, brash, and, for better or worse, he made people pay attention. Some saw a savior. Others saw chaos. But me? I saw a warning: we're starving for leadership that isn't either extreme.

We need a leader who is young enough to care about the future and wise enough to honor the past. I'm 32 now. In three years, I could legally run for president. That's wild. But honestly—maybe someone like me should run. Not because I want the power, but because I want to remind people to slow down and listen. To think about the *Colors of the Wind*, not just the color of someone's skin or political party.

On Race, Immigration, and Responsibility

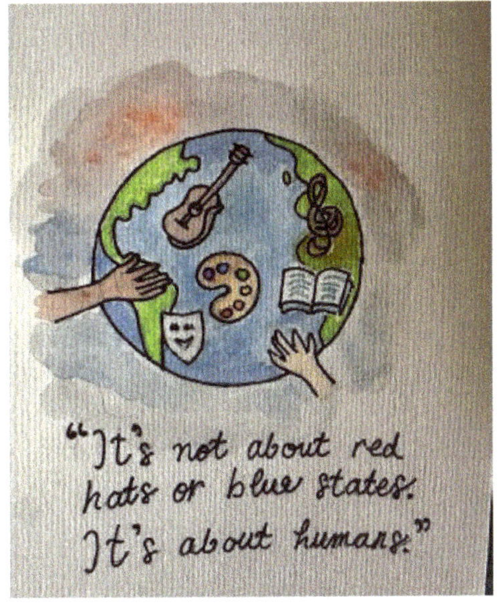

Let's be real. White people have history, too—some painful, some shameful. But so does every group. We can't heal if we're constantly tearing open wounds. Instead, we need empathy and understanding.

I don't believe in deporting hard-working immigrants who love this country and provide for their families. If someone is building a life, contributing to society, and doing the right thing—they deserve a chance at the American dream too. It's not about red hats or blue states. It's about humans.

Let's also stop punishing success. Tax the rich? Maybe. But don't choke out the very businesses that hire, feed, and create. Artists are small business owners too. We build slowly and from scratch—just like farmers, builders, and ranchers. Creativity thrives in freedom, not fear. And let's not push landowners into a corner with skyrocketing property taxes. We need land. We need farmers. We need horsemen and horsewomen. And yes, we need people who still believe the Earth is sacred.

Back to the Wind

I go back to *Pocahontas* a lot. That song *Colors of the Wind*—it wasn't just about a girl and a tree. It was about understanding people, respecting nature, and listening before you judge. We need more of that today.

We don't need to agree on everything. But we do need to slow down. Observe. Create. Listen. Lead.

Because in this world of noise and war and sides—we forget to live.

And I don't want to forget.

I want to keep creating anyway.

"Creativity is intelligence having fun."
— *Albert Einstein*

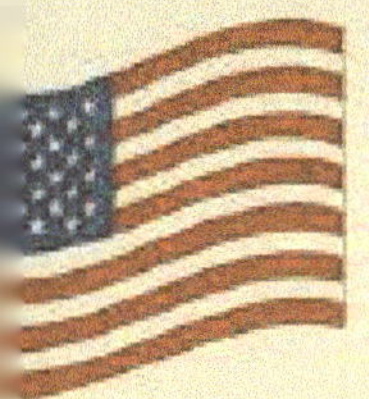
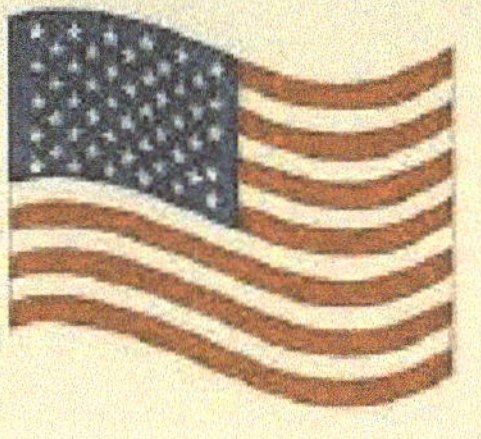

CHAPTER 17

WHY NOT ME?

(A PRESIDENCY DAYDREAM)

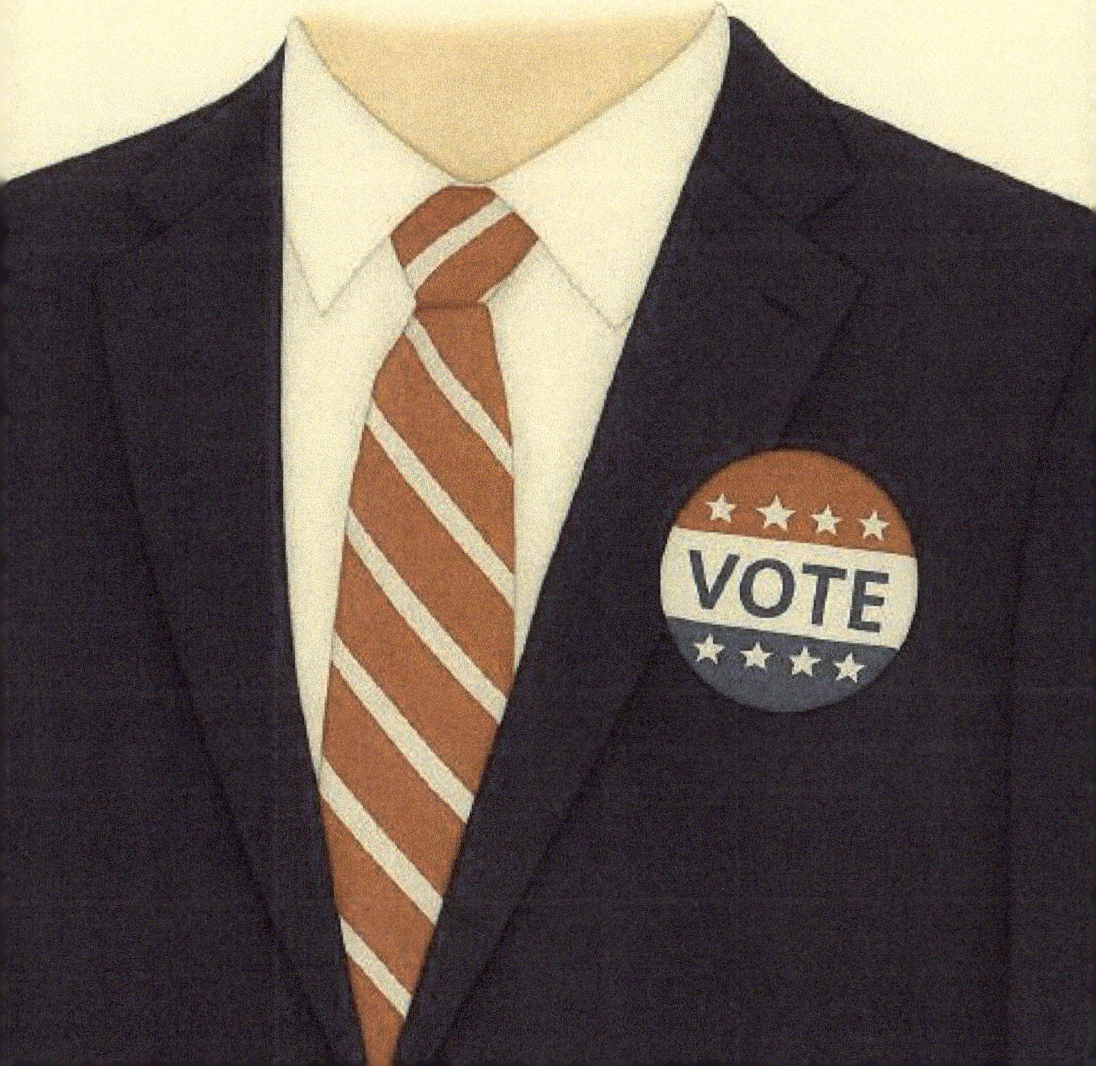

~

"One day, I asked myself a question out loud — What if I ran for president?"

Not because I had the perfect plan or a political degree. But because I started to believe that leaders shouldn't just be career politicians. Maybe leaders can be artists. Farmers. Builders. Daughters. Dreamers.

I've never fit one mold — so why should my path to leadership be any different?

Would I get enough support from my family? Maybe. Some would cheer, some might laugh. Would my friends get it? Probably more than I expected. Would strangers vote for someone who still believes in painting sunsets, feeding chickens, and singing the national anthem with pride and tears in her eyes?

Maybe. Maybe not. But the point is: I'd still try.

What Would My Campaign Sound Like?

Slogan: *Keep Creating Anyway — A New Vision for America*

Core Belief: *Creativity is courage. Leadership is listening.*

Vice President: *Someone who tells the truth, even when it's hard. Someone calm when I'm fiery. Steady when I soar.*

Platform: *Protect nature. Honor tradition. Build futures. Empower them every day.*

How Do You Run for President?

Basic Requirements

- Be a natural-born U.S. citizen
- Be at least 35 years old
- Have lived in the U.S. for at least 14 years

Steps to Run

- File paperwork with the Federal Election Commission (FEC)
- Build a campaign team
- Raise funds
- Get on the ballot in all 50 states
- Participate in debates & primaries (if part of a political party)
- Win the Electoral College

What I'd Run On

- **Art & Education Access:** Creativity belongs in every classroom.
- **Mental Health Advocacy:** Slow down, breathe, and live well.
- **Land, Legacy & Local:** Support small farms and local makers.
- **Modern Diplomacy:** Less ego, more empathy.
- **Youthful Leadership:** Imagination is not immaturity — it's power.

Would I really run someday?

Maybe. Maybe not.

But the daydream reminds me:

"You can lead with kindness, and still be strong."

But here's the real secret: you start by believing you're allowed to lead.

And that's where my story begins. Whether or not I ever run, I know one thing — every day, we each get the chance to lead our own lives like they matter.

Final Thought:

So maybe I won't ever be in the Oval Office. But I will keep building homes, raising cattle, painting life, and showing up with love. That's my kind of presidency.

Because the truth is —

you don't need a podium to lead.

You just need purpose.

CHAPTER 18

PEACE IS SOMETHING WE CREATE

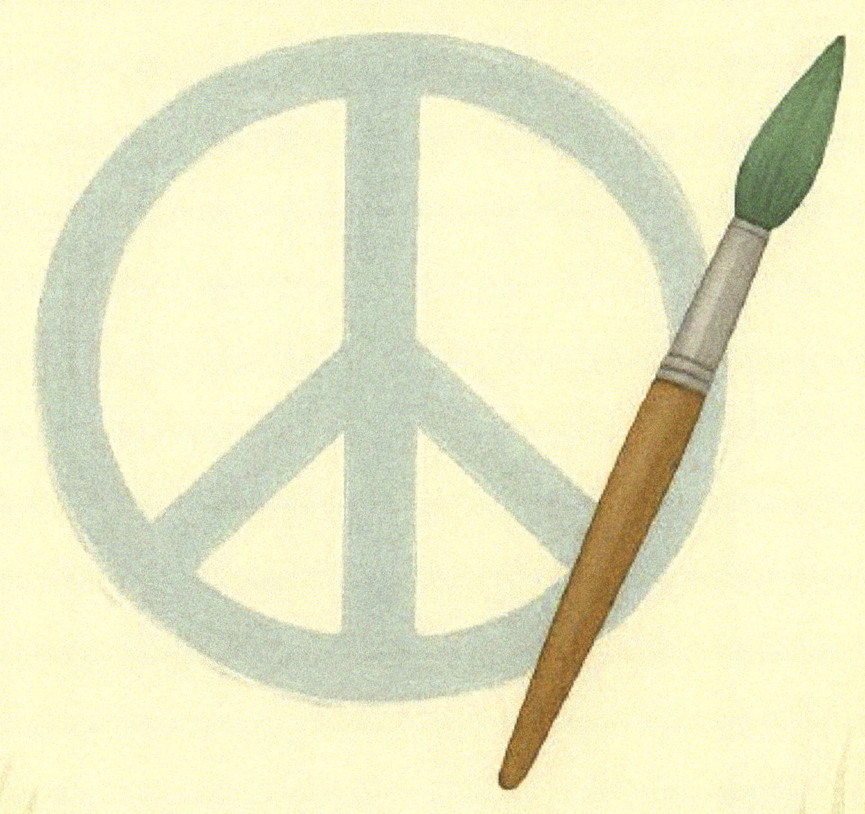

Foreign policy through a creative lens

~

I used to think politics was for people with perfect speeches and pressed suits. But the more I lived — on farms, under paintbrushes, through heartbreak and headlines — the more I realized:

We are all already leaders.

Some of us lead with laws. Some with stories. Some with color.

Some lead armies. Some raise kids. Some raise cattle.

But leadership isn't about power. It's about vision.

And if I had the chance to lead — not just a business, not just a movement, but a country — here's what I would say to the world:

Foreign Policy, the Creative Way

When the world gets louder with conflict, I believe we should answer with both strength and soul. With action — and with imagination. Because peace doesn't happen by accident. Peace is something we have to create.

Ukraine: Defend the Dreamers

The people of Ukraine didn't ask for war — but they rose to it with resilience, music, murals, and unimaginable strength.

In my America, we defend dreamers, not destroyers. We fund aid, not escalation. We back borders, but also brushstrokes.

Because if you can still create art in a war zone, you deserve the world's support.

Iran: Stand for the Voices They Try to Silence

In Iran, women are risking their lives for a simple idea: freedom. For voice. For education. For beauty.

And I believe America should listen louder. Not just with sanctions, but with support. Not just in press conferences, but in poems, protests, and paint.

We stand with the women of Iran — because their fight is our fight.

Foreign Policy as a Creative Act

I don't just want to protect buildings.

I want to protect books.

I want to protect songs.

I want to protect color and faith and freedom.

So if I ever stood behind that podium with the seal of the United States, I wouldn't just quote policy. I'd quote purpose.

CHAPTER 19

THE POWER PERSONAL STYLE

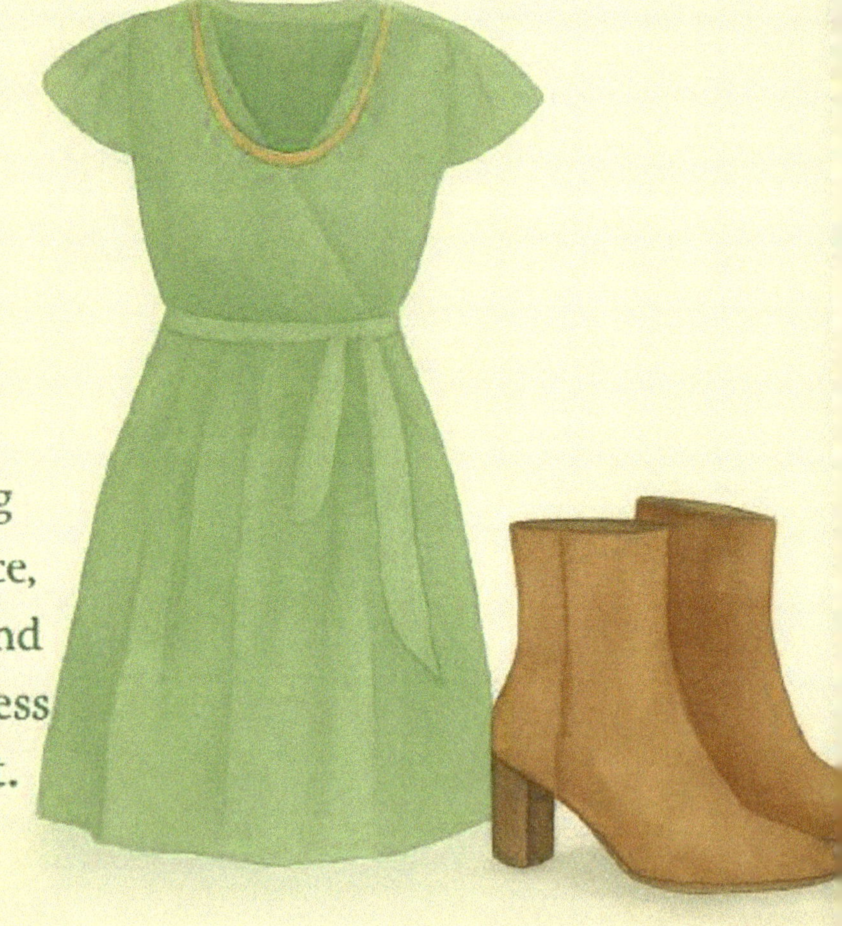

Exploring visual voice, identity, and how to dress the part.

~

"You think I'm an ignorant savage...
And you've been so many places, I guess it must be so." – Pocahontas

That line stayed with me for years. Not because of how it was said—but because of why it was said.

Pocahontas didn't yell. She wanted to be demanding. She was simply showing someone the depth of what they couldn't see: identity, intuition, and connection to the path that had been dismissed.

That's what personal style is. It's what we wear. How we speak. How we move through a room. But most importantly—it's what we believe in, reflected outward.

What you wear isn't just fashion—it's a feeling.

For me, style has always been more about mood than trend. My favorite outfit might be breezy, lined with boots covered in studio dust. It might be a silk scarf tied like a ribbon, or a ranch hat tossed in the front seat of my truck.

But it all says something.

It says: I care about where I've come from—and where I'm headed.

It says: I can be rugged and refined. Coastal and cowgirl. Artful and grounded.

It took me time to understand that our style evolves with our self-trust. The more I grew into who I was, the less I needed outside approval to decide what felt "right."

Visual Voice & Branding: A Personal Language

My art changed too. The colors got bolder. The texture is richer. The subjects are more personal. When I started Nina Barr Studio, I didn't just want a logo—I wanted a visual voice.

One that says:

- "This girl grew up with cattle and a camera."
- "She sees the world in color but notices the quiet details."
- "Her art is personal, but it speaks to something universal."

From the layout of a gallery to the fonts I use on Instagram, everything became part of my evolving self-expression.

That's branding—but it's also soul work.

Presidential Style: Power in Presentation

Let's talk about presidents. Yes—really.

When I wrote *Chapter 13: Why Not Me?* I joked about running for president one day. But the deeper message was this: every president had a signature. A story. A presence.

- Lincoln's hat
- JFK's clean confidence
- Obama's charisma and cool tone
- Even Washington's statuesque silence
- Trump's signature Coca-Cola button

They knew the power of how they were seen—and how that shaped what they said.

If I ever did run (hypothetically or creatively), I know exactly what I'd wear:

- A green dress for growth
- Boots that show I've walked through mud and made something from it
- A subtle necklace passed down from someone who believes in me

Because that would say it all—without saying a word.

Style as a Sign of Growth

Your personal style isn't fixed. It grows with you.

What I wore when I was insecure is not what I wear now. What I posted when I needed validation is not what I share now.

Your palette changes.

Your language evolves.

Your self-respect deepens.

Style, at its core, is your soul learning to speak in visuals.

Closing Reflection

Pocahontas taught me that power doesn't always roar.

Sometimes it whispers.

Sometimes it sings.

Sometimes it paints or poses for photographs.

And sometimes, it just walks into a room fully aware of who she is.

So whether it's in your boots, your brushstrokes, or your branding—

Let your style speak.

Let it grow. Let it reflect who you've become.

Because that is not just fashion.

That's freedom.

CHAPTER 20

TIKTOK, TIMELINES, & TIDES

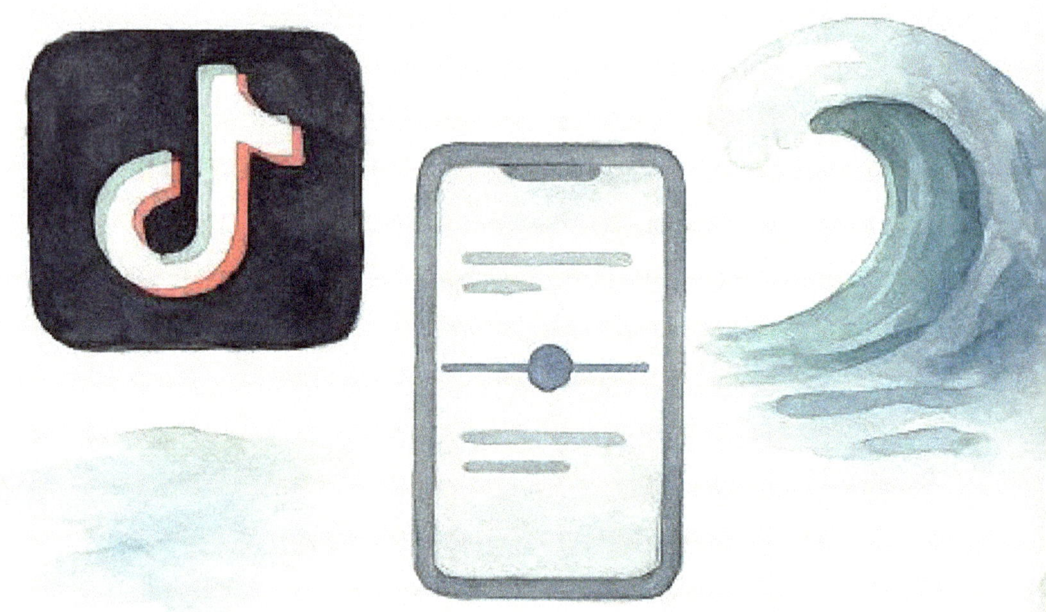

How trends rise and fall, but the truth remains – and so does your voice.

~

"It's easy to go viral.

It's harder to stay grounded."

During the stillness of COVID, I started posting on TikTok. No real plan. No idea what would happen. Just videos of my art, some animal moments, small scenes from a life I was slowly learning to love.

And then—like most things online—one of them blew up. Suddenly, I had views, comments, and attention. It felt exciting. Validation, even. But here's the truth: **that wasn't the point.**

The Digital Artist's Dilemma

Social media is powerful—but it can also pull you in too deep. You start asking:

Am I creating from my heart? Or just for the algorithm?

Would I still paint if no one saw it?

The real challenge isn't going viral. It's being **seen and still staying yourself.**

I've learned to use these platforms as tools—not mirrors. I post when I feel proud. I share when it's honest. And if I need a break, I take one.

Tides of Truth

Creativity moves like the ocean. There are seasons of high energy and long, quiet pauses. There are waves of interest and moments of still water. But that doesn't mean the current has stopped.

Sometimes a post will land flat... and a week later, the same energy will circle back in a commission, a client, or a compliment from a stranger who really saw the work.

That's why I keep creating anyway. Because I'd rather post my truth than chase approval. I'd rather make work I love than ride a trend I don't believe in.

Staying Grounded

The best thing I will ever do for my creative life—is to get outside. Touch the dirt. Pet the animals. And breathe.

My horses, my dogs, the Florida sky, a walk in the field—all of it reminds me of what matters. I found myself in the real world so I don't lose myself in the digital one.

Even Pocahontas whispers this wisdom:

"Listen with your heart, you will understand."

So I do. I listen to the land.

I slow down.

And I remember that success, just like the tide, always finds its way back if you're aligned with purpose.

My Platform is Bigger than the App

My work doesn't just live on social media. It lives in my sketchbooks. In my studio. On my clients' walls. It lives in markets, shows, barns, and sunlit galleries.

My platform is the lens.

The canvas.

The ground I stand on.

And even if the apps go silent, I'll still be here—creating with my hand and my heart.

Final Thought

Viral moments come and go.

Trends rise, fall, repeat.

But the truth?

That stays.

So no matter what the numbers say, I'll keep showing up.

One brushstroke at a time.

One post at a time.

One peaceful tide at a time.

When the room is silent, keep painting anyway.

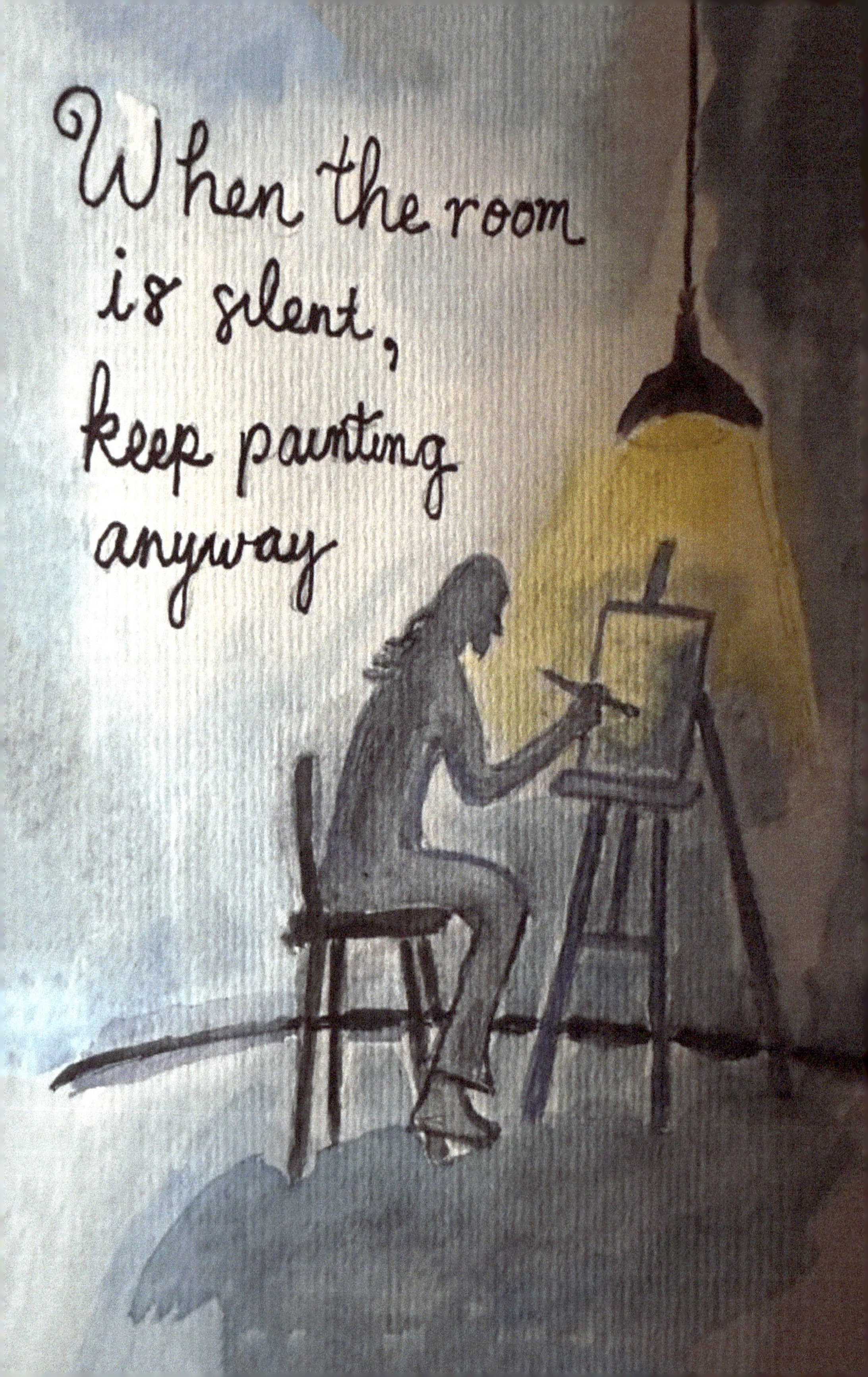

When the room
is silent,
keep painting
anyway

Because this isn't about fame.

This is about soul work.

And that?

That always lasts.

Part VI:
Keep Creating Anyway

CHAPTER 21

WHEN NOBODY CLAPS

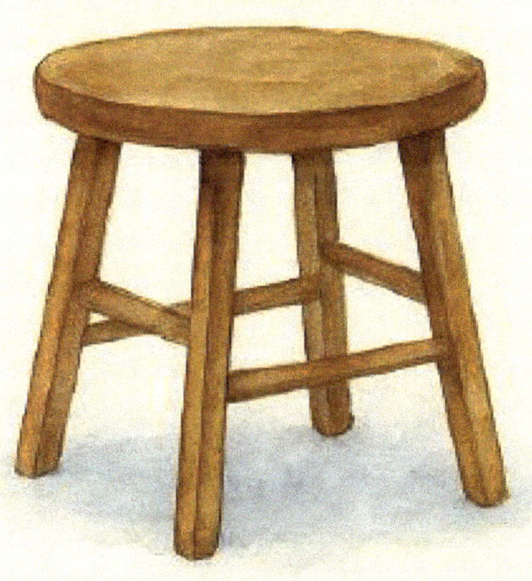

Making art for yourself,
Instead of an applause.

~

There's something sacred about creating when no one's watching. No followers, no likes, no applause. Just you and the quiet rhythm of making something new.

It's the brush dipping into water. The soft click of a shutter. The slow swirl of pencil on a blank page.

That's where the real magic lives.

Sure, it's exciting when something sells, when the world finally hears it. When the work is recognized.

But the deepest joy? It doesn't live at the finish line.

It lives in the process. In the trying.

The moment you're so lost in what you're doing, the rest of the world fades away.

That's joy.

That's art.

That's the point.

When Nobody Claps

I used to think success meant applause. I thought the work had to be seen, validated, even celebrated to matter.

But the more I create, the more I realize the truth: the most meaningful things I've made were born in silence.

No audience. No feedback. Just pure expression.

Sometimes no one claps.

Sometimes no one sees it at all.

But I made it anyway.

Because joy doesn't wait for a crowd. Joy shows up in the making.

It's Not About Perfection

I've said this before, and I'll say it again: your art doesn't have to be perfect to be powerful.

The joy isn't in getting it right.

It's showing up.

It's in the crooked brushstroke, the unexpected curve, the glorious mess that becomes a masterpiece simply because you made it with your heart.

Some days I don't finish anything. Some days I just sit in my studio, pet the dogs, sip a second cup of coffee, and stare at the light changing across the room— and that's still part of it.

Being present is part of it. Listening to the world around you is part of it. Letting yourself breathe, rest, and return—still counts as creating.

A Quiet Kind of Victory

Success isn't always loud. Sometimes it's the soft smile you give yourself when something finally feels right. Or the peace of knowing you created something beautiful that nobody else needed to understand.

This chapter isn't a how-to.

It's a reminder:

You don't need a gallery show to be an artist.

You don't need to go viral to be valuable.

You don't need applause to be enough.

You just need to keep creating.

Even when nobody claps.

Especially when nobody claps.

Because of the joy?

The real joy?

It's in the making.

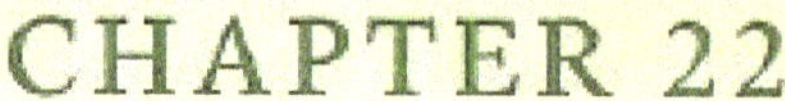

CHAPTER 22

LETTERS I NEVER SENT

The things I never said, but always meant.

~

Some words stay stuck inside us. Not because they're weak, but because they're weighty. Because if we said them out loud, the world might shift. Or maybe—we would.

Letters I wrote in my head on long walks, during quiet drives, or while cleaning paintbrushes. Letters I never mailed. But I need to write.

This chapter is a collection of those words I never mailed. The words I wrote to myself, and to those who shaped me—whether they stayed or didn't.

Dear Art Teacher Who Told Me My Art Was Good

There were many of you. From sketching in the old Wellington Mall, to the classroom corner in elementary school, to high school where art was always my favorite subject—you saw something in me before I fully saw it in myself.

You said I had potential.

And I held on to that.

This is a reminder: I stuck with it.

I'm still creating.

And I made it—because someone once believed in me.

Thank you.

Dear Younger Me

You were never behind.

You didn't miss it.

You didn't take too long.

You were just growing. Becoming.

Even the quiet season had purpose.

Even the "What am I doing?" moments shaped something inside you.

You kept showing up—even when the path wasn't clear.

I'm proud of you.

Keep going.

To the Friends Who Came and Went

Look at me now.

We had good times, wild times, bad times—and everything in between.

And even though not all of you stayed, you helped me grow.

You helped me learn that I don't have to be liked by everyone.

That not every friendship is forever—but every one of them meant something.

To the Guys I Dated, Loved, or Almost Loved

Relationships. Situationships. Flirtations.

This is for all of them.

You might not have seen the full version of me back then—but she was already becoming something strong.

Maybe you wish you stayed.

Maybe you don't.

Either way…

Look at me now.

Dear My Family

To every single one of you—thank you.

For shaping me, supporting me, challenging me, loving me.

Family isn't always easy, but it's always part of who we are.

You gave me roots, my stories, my grit, and my heart.

You've been there for the milestones—and the messes.

You've seen me through every phase, and still stood by me as I figured it out.

Whether we talk every day or only once in a while—your presence is felt.

This journey isn't just mine. It's ours.

Dear Future Me

I hope you still create like no one's watching.

I hope you still let the sun hit your canvas and the dogs sit by your side.

I hope you laugh more, worry less, and never stop dreaming.

And I hope—most of all—you're proud of everything it took to get here.

Thank you.

These are the letters I never sent.

Maybe you send some too.

Write them.

Hold them.

And keep going.

CHAPTER 23

WHAT IF I DO IT ANYWAY?

A quiet dare to myself –
and maybe to you, too.

~

What if I try?

What if I fail?

What if I look silly, or don't get the job, or people talk behind my back?

But also—

What if I don't try?

What if I never knew what I was capable of because I was too afraid to find out?

What if I do it anyway?

The Voice of Doubt

It always starts small:

"That's not realistic."

"That's already been done."

"You're not good enough."

But here's what I've learned: that voice is a liar. Or at least—it's trying to keep me safe, not successful. It confuses comfort with creativity.

You don't build a life by listening to fear. You build it by taking the next step. Even when it shakes.

I've Been Told "NO"

I've been told I wasn't ready.

My work isn't strong enough.

That I should have a backup plan.

But every "no" was a spark—

Because it taught me to bet on myself anyway.

If you're reading this and thinking, *yeah, but...* let me interrupt you:

Do it anyway.

The Leap Is Worth It

I'm not saying it's always easy. It's not.

Sometimes you leap and land in mud.

But sometimes—sometimes—you fly.

And nothing feels better than proving to yourself that you could.

That you did.

So, What If You Do It Anyway?

What if you start a business?

Take the trip?

Write the book?

Paint the piece?

Send the email?

Send a letter?

Say the thing?

What if you look back a year from now and say,

"I'm so glad I didn't wait."

You don't need permission.

You don't need a perfect plan.

You don't need everything figured out.

You just need to start.

Because what if it doesn't go away?

But one day, they all become stories.

And I hope yours begins with:

"I was scared. But I did it anyway."

You'll Hear a Lot of Voices in Your Life

Some will cheer you on.

Others will whisper doubt.

And some will flat-out tell you that your dreams are too risky, too expensive, too unrealistic.

They'll say things like:

"You haven't earned it."

"You're just an employee."

"It's not your property."

"No one makes money doing that."

"Be practical."

"Don't ask too much."

I've heard all of that—and more.

But here's what they don't understand:

This isn't just about money.

Or buildings.

Or proving someone wrong.

This is about purpose.

It's about doing the work your heart keeps pulling you toward—even when it doesn't make sense on paper.

Because dreams aren't always logical.

Sometimes they're messy. Bold. Emotional. Faith-driven.

And most of the time? They're built with nothing but grit, sketchbooks, late nights, and *what if* questions.

The Fear of Asking

They say I'm asking for too much—

Too much time, too much help, too much space.

But what they don't see is that I'm not just asking.

I'm building.

I'm learning to be the kind of person who takes ownership of their story—even if it's on land I didn't buy, or in a studio I haven't built yet.

If I wait for everyone's permission, I'll never begin.

If I wait for everyone to see the vision, I'll never finish.

So yes, I might build a barn.

Yes, I might expand the ranch.

Yes, I might keep creating even when nobody claps.

A Word to Anyone Who's Been Dismissed

If someone's ever told you that you're easily replaceable,

That you don't bring value,

That you're "just" an employee, "just" a kid with an idea,

That your dream is unrealistic—

Do it anyway.

Even if it fails.

Even if it scares you.

Even if it means starting over a hundred times.

Because in the end, what matters most is not what they think.

It's what you choose to do with the time, talent, and vision you've been given.

The Last Word

Maybe it's not about the barn, the land, or the numbers.

Maybe it's about building a life that makes sense to you—

With horses, paintbrushes, and stubborn hope.

With truth, not titles.

With work that feeds your spirit, not just your bank account.

So if you're waiting for a sign—

This is it.

Do it anyway.

And then?

Keep creating.

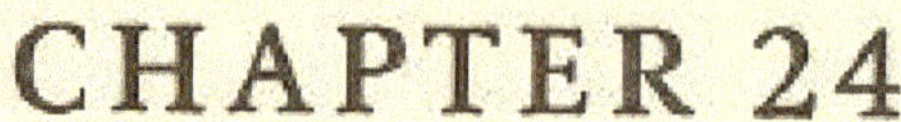

CHAPTER 24

WHAT WE LEAVE BEHIND

A Legacy Letter to the Ones Who Come Next

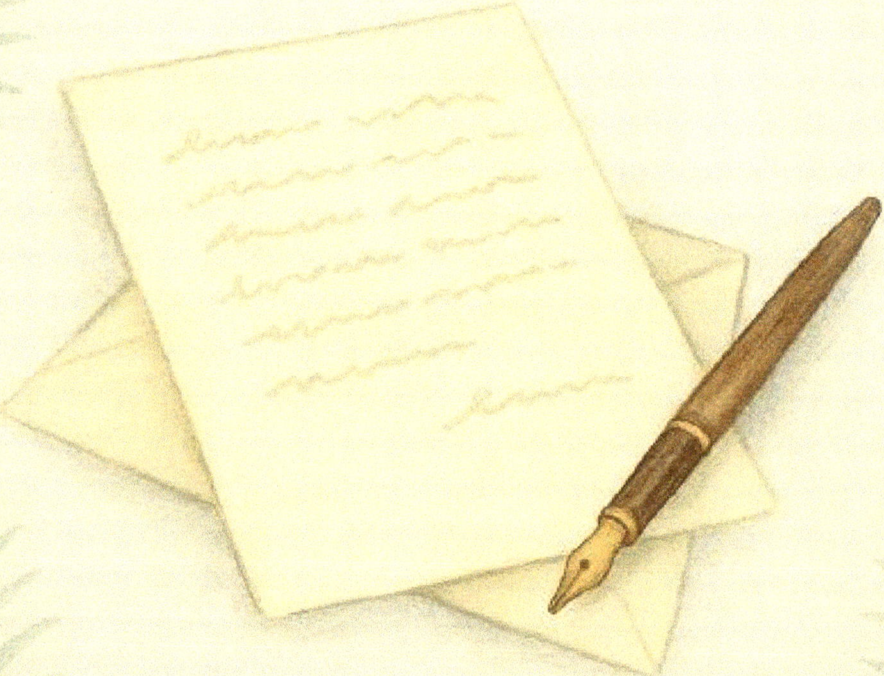

~

If you've made it to this chapter, thank you.

Not just for reading—but for walking beside me.

This book has been a winding path through art and heartbreak, dreams and detours, paint and purpose.

And now, as it closes, I want to speak directly to the future.

To the ones just getting started.

To the girl with chalk on her hands.

To the boy sketching horses in the margins of his notebook.

To the teen who feels like no one understands their weird, wonderful brain.

To the adult wondering if they're too late.

You're not too late.

You're right on time.

What We Pass On

We don't get to choose how long we're here.

But we do get to choose how brightly we burn.

How deeply we care.

How bravely we create.

And that's the legacy I want to leave:

That art matters.

That stories matter.

That you don't have to be famous to be fulfilled.

You just have to be honest. And open. And willing to begin.

The Kids Who'll Come After

Maybe one day a little girl will find this book on her mom's shelf.

Maybe she'll flip through it and see photos, brushstrokes, and truths that make her feel less alone.

Maybe she'll start to draw.

Or build.

Or dream something entirely new.

If that happens—just once—I'll have done my job.

A Thank You Note

To every person who ever told me to keep going—thank you.

To every person who didn't believe in me—thank you, too. You taught me to believe in myself.

To the teachers, the dogs, the farmers, the artists, the long walks, the bad dates, the quiet mornings, the late nights in the studio—you made this possible.

To you, the reader: I hope you feel seen.

I hope you feel brave.

And I hope you feel ready.

A Permission Slip

This is your permission to create.

To mess up.

To start over.

To feel joy.

To cry sometimes.

To make something that didn't exist before.

You don't need anyone else to say you're worthy.

You already are.

So keep drawing.

Keep dreaming.

Keep creating.

Anyways,

—Nina

I want to keep creating anyway

Acknowledgements

To the land – for grounding me.

To the animals – for keeping me present.

To the ones who believed in me while I was still figuring it out – thank you.

To my family – your grit, heart, and honesty made me who I am.

To every artist who doubted themselves but kept creating anyway – this book is for you.

And finally, to the readers: thank you for letting me share this piece of my world.

May it remind you to slow down, show up, and live creatively – on your terms.

About the Author

Nina Barr is a multidisciplinary artist, photographer, and writer based in South Florida. Raised on the land and shaped by both ranch life and creative pursuit, she blends earth and art in every piece she creates.

Through her studio, Nina Barr Studio, she captures the beauty of slow living – drawing inspiration from horses, ocean tides, and honest moments.

Keep Creating Anyway is her debut book – a narrative memoir-meets-manifesto for anyone learning to trust their pace, honor their story, and create with heart.

www.ingramcontent.com/pod-product-compliance
Ingram Content Group UK Ltd.
Pitfield, Milton Keynes, MK11 3LW, UK
UKHW062301290726
14090UKWH00017B/826

9 781807 210212